MORTIFICATION
Eight Deaths and Life After Them

Also by Mark Watson

FICTION
Contacts
The Place That Didn't Exist
Hotel Alpha
The Knot
Eleven
A Light-Hearted Look at Murder
Bullet Points

GRAPHIC FICTION
Dan and Sam (with Oliver Harud)

MORTIFICATION

Eight Deaths and Life After Them

Mark Watson

PHOENIX

First published in Great Britain in 2023 by Phoenix Books,
an imprint of The Orion Publishing Group Ltd
Carmelite House, 50 Victoria Embankment
London EC4Y 0DZ

An Hachette UK Company

1 3 5 7 9 10 8 6 4 2

A CIP catalogue record for this book is
available from the British Library.

A version of this book was published as an Audible Original in 2021
under the title *8 Deaths (and Life After Them)*

ISBN (Hardback) 978 1 3996 0768 1
ISBN (Export Trade Paperback) 978 1 39960 771 1
ISBN (eBook) 978 1 39960 770 4

Typeset by Input Data Services Ltd, Bridgwater, Somerset

Printed in Great Britain by Clays Ltd, Elcograf S.p.A.

www.orionbooks.co.uk
www.phoenix-books.co.uk

Contents

Mum and Dad: this is dedicated to you both, but I'm sort of hoping you don't read it.

PROLOGUE:

WINNING AT LIFE

Being a human, one among billions in a vast strange universe, is a big challenge. If you don't think enough about what you're doing with your life, you run the risk of making huge, disastrous errors. If you think *too* much about it, the range of possibilities overwhelms you so much that you can't do anything except sit eating toast and whimpering (and even then, the selection of spreads available is enough to cause further anguish). Life is the most complicated gift you'll ever receive, but – as people often say – it comes with no instruction manual.

Except, these days, it can. Into this void, this yearning we all feel for advice and direction, have stepped many people who claim they can tell you how to 'win at life'. The implication is that they themselves are winners, life experts who – like experts in tennis, or dieting, or sheep-shearing – can make you a winner, too.

To me, making a claim like this seems an incredibly rash act of fate-tempting, given what we all know about how quickly life can turn sour when things seem to be going well: a topic that has been widely covered in art and literature, most famously by the Greek tragedies and Alanis Morissette in the song 'Ironic'. (Greek tragedies often include the line, 'Call no man happy until he is dead', which sums the situation up pretty efficiently, but doesn't always go down well at dinner parties.) Sometimes – no matter how white and shiny your teeth on your Twitter avatar or how many adoring retweets rack up for your description of a low-calorie lunch – there are going to be days when you do *not* win. Sometimes weeks. To pretend otherwise is to imply that you have access to some special immunity which no human can attain.

Much more damagingly, the idea that it is possible to 'win at life' promotes a mentality which is more binary and simplistic than our experiences ever can be. If you're playing in a football match or entering your puppy in a dog show you will know by the end whether you have won or lost (although, weirdly, the puppy itself probably won't). But life isn't a dog show and it isn't a massively long game of football, either, however much I might enjoy that. There is no giant scoreboard above our heads as we walk around; in the final moments of your life, you will not be given a report card with grades on it. Our lives are to be enjoyed for what they are, not squeezed and contorted into endless different shapes to meet arbitrary goals we identify for ourselves.

This is not something I've always known. It is something I learned the hard way, by *trying* to 'win at life'. By devoting swathes of my time, energy and passion to chasing victories throughout my twenties and thirties, and falling short: often publicly, often in ways that undermined my sense of who I was. Whatever I now know about life – or think I know – I found out through failure, disappointment, mortification.

On 13 February 2020 – my fortieth birthday – I was reflecting on this, in the spirit of reflection we sometimes embark on during birthdays, especially if 'we' (I) have had some red wine. I pondered the many setbacks and embarrassments that had littered the road from birth to middle age; the many times that road had not taken me in the direction I imagined it would.

Over the course of the pages that follow, you'll hear how I made errors which cost me career opportunities that would never come round again; became dependent on psychological props that weren't sustainable; drank too heavily; isolated people around me; became a substandard father, husband, friend and professional; sank to a vantage point from which my life seemed of so little value that I questioned whether to carry on with it. And yet here I still was. I had survived these reversals. I might not be on the path I expected, but I was still moving forward, all the same. The idea of writing a book like this entered my head for the first time: not as a manual for success, but a handbook for accepting, and moving on from, the opposite. Not as a victory lap, but as a chronicle of a battle against life's many setbacks.

If you took note of that date, you'll know what happened next. Barely a month after my birthday party took place, the venue had closed its doors permanently, and many of the guests were gone from my life for the next two years. To be clear, this is not because of my behaviour at the party. What happened in the month after my fortieth was, as I'm sure you'll remember whenever you are reading this, unprecedented. If nothing else, you'll remember because the word 'unprecedented' was on every TV and radio broadcast from there until Christmas. Schools shut; careers were put on hold; friends and families were estranged. Whatever worldly knowledge I might have stacked up was as useless as anybody else's, with the exception of government health adviser Chris Whitty, who became the most (and only) sought-after 'performer' in the UK. Any 'rules for life' I had gleaned from all the ups and downs seemed to have been rendered moot; they made no more sense than continuing to move the Monopoly hat around the table after someone had taken the board away.

But the pandemic receded, bit by bit, and life regained something like its old shape. I was able to get back to touring again, to travelling around the country – even, sometimes, beyond our borders. I continued, though, to spend a lot of time interacting with the online audience I'd built up during my various attempts to keep some form of comedy going in lockdown. It was noticeable that, although we might have many of our freedoms back, the psychological effects of the long, strange pandemic period were felt everywhere. Some people's work had dried up for good. Others found it impossible to focus on what used to be their jobs, even if they *could* return to them. Lots of people had come to feel, during the isolation and introspection of the lockdowns, that their relationships or careers or ambitions weren't the right ones, but weren't sure what to replace them with.

More people than I had ever been aware of before seemed to feel – in a word – lost. I recognised those feelings from the many, many times I had been blown off course. I started to think again that perhaps I had something I could usefully share. Not because I had got life figured out, or was 'winning' at it. But because I knew that I hadn't, and perhaps never would.

The thing outsiders most commonly say about stand-up comedy is how brave you must have to be to do it; how it would be their 'worst nightmare'. All comedians have had this said to them by somebody who's quite clearly done much more nightmarish things. My best one is the famous neurosurgeon, Henry Marsh, whom I met at a radio recording. The first chapter of his memoir *Do No Harm* describes how cutting into the brain never stops being, on an objective level, absolutely horrifying. Forty years of opening up people's skulls, knowing that the slightest slip will destroy at least one life. And yet just before we went on stage, he said to me, 'Being a comedian must be absolutely terrifying.'

When people talk about the bravery of comedians, I always tell them that I'd almost certainly be more scared to do whatever their job is than I am to do my own. This is obviously true if they have some sort of high-stakes gig like a pilot or a bomb disposal expert or if they defuse bombs *while* flying planes (the sort of employment in which you might see Nicolas Cage on screen if you were too tired to get up and change the channel). But it's equally true of pretty much anything workers do from day to day.

Anything you do in life has the potential to beat you up, shred your self-esteem, send you back to the drawing board again and again, make you wonder why you bothered. But it *is* true to say that, in comedy, these things can happen several times a week, in front of a lot of other people. There aren't many jobs in which 'death' is used as a synonym for, 'Well, that didn't go very well.' You have to be a particular type of person to put yourself in that situation. To sign up to die over and over again.

I am not presenting myself as someone who has accumulated a great storehouse of worldly wisdom and is generously allowing the reader to join a guided tour. It would be truer to say that I have learned some lessons and am, permanently, in the process of trying to remember and act upon them.

Rather than a game with winners or losers, I've come to think we should see life as a piece of music. There'll be unexpected changes of tempo, lulls and strange, violent moments that you didn't anticipate – but they are all part of the tune, and the trick is to dance along with it. When I say 'I've come to think', I mean that I stole this idea from the work of my entertainment hero Derren Brown, who mentioned it in one of his shows (we'll come back to this). The analogy has its limits, not least because I cannot dance and the thought of doing it in public fills me with horror. But perhaps there's something to learn even from *that*. 'Dance like nobody's watching,' fridge magnets like to advise. What if you lived like nobody was judging?

Mortifications, of all kinds, are only as important as we allow them to be. Other people's opinions are just that: other people's. Your life is your own, and you are only accountable to yourself. It has taken me what will probably prove to be more than half of my time on earth to absorb that idea, and, even now, I disregard it constantly.

Perhaps I'm hoping that by writing all this down, I'll absorb whatever emotional nutrients are in it myself, as well as sharing them with other people. Maybe I'm writing this for me as much as for any other reader. As a reminder of some of the places I've been mentally and the ways I might avoid going there again. But now that you have read this far, I'd really like you to stick around. No performance is much fun if nobody shows up to watch. Believe me: on that score, I know what I'm talking about.

I

WHAT'S IT LIKE WHEN YOU DIE?

'What's it like when you die?' It's not a question you can pose to many groups in society. Off the top of my head, I'd say you've got: stand-up comedians, ghosts and people who have seen a bright light on an operating table and claim to have looked away from it because it 'wasn't the right time'. The second and third of these categories are in fairly short supply. But comedians are everywhere, and every single one of us has an answer to that question. We knew you were going to ask it.

As soon as you're outed in public as a stand-up – at a party, or in the back of a taxi – you have a good idea of how the conversation will go. First, your questioner will say that they're 'rubbish with names' and try to establish exactly why they recognise you. In my very specific case, they will often compliment a couple of pieces of work which reveal that they have mistaken me for the actor, Chris O'Dowd. Then your questioner will move on to give you a rundown of all the comedians they've ever seen and what they thought of them. If they're a more opinionated sort, they might do this in the form of a test – asking, 'What do you make of that Sarah Millican? That fella Micky Flanagan, do you reckon he's funny?' – before telling you whether you were right or not.

A couple of minutes in (if you haven't succeeded in steering the talk to *their* profession) they will ask you how you got into comedy in the first place, and why you wanted to, when – as we've established – it is their personal idea of hell. This second query, however, is really just building towards the one they are keenest to ask. 'What do you do about hecklers?' And, finally, there it is: the death question.

I usually say something generic like, 'Ha, it happens to everyone; it's part of how you learn!' But if this was a conversation in a movie, you would at this point see my eyes cloud over, perhaps hear a sort of record scratch. You would know we were now in a flashback. The present-day me at the party, or in the taxi, would dissolve into a clean-shaven, even scrawnier but less weather-beaten version.

This Mark Watson is standing on a stage in Maidstone, Kent. A caption comes up. 'Friday, 9 April 2004.' That's right: 2004. I'd love to maintain that I'm not haunted by a performance that took place not far off twenty years ago, but the truth is: ghosts are everywhere. If you're going to get to know me at all, there's no point in pretending that mine have all been exorcised, or busted, to use the modern procedural term. I live with my past all the time.

It's been a long slog to shake some of those spirits off; others are ever-present.

This younger, more naive version of me is standing on a stage, in the third year of what he hopes will become a comedy career, doing much the same thing as he always has: a five-minute comedy set which has served him well in competitions, open mics, all the way up to appearances in busy weekend comedy clubs like this one. But tonight, and for the first time, he's in big trouble.

With hindsight, there have been one or two warning signs. The show is starting very late, because of traffic problems nearby. This has given the already drunk, aggressive and largely bald crowd the opportunity to get drunker and more aggressive (although probably not any balder). There is a certain apprehension in the green room, alongside the more familiar atmosphere of the place: deodorant, old beer, and disappointed comedians who are the sort of men you might, these days, glimpse in pubs saying things like, 'It's gone too far the other way, hasn't it?', because there's women's football on TV. Not the sort of place where many people in their mid-twenties would hang out on a Friday night, that's for sure. But, to an aspiring comedian, very much the sort of ambience that makes you think: I am on the verge of making it. This is what I wanted. The late start and the rising noise of the punters do not faze me. I'm ready for this.

An aspiring comedian: that's what I am, at the age of twenty-four, in this flashback. I have no idea that those aspirations will appear idiotic in just a couple of hours. We are approaching the part of the movie where the Wall Street banker and his wife stand on the porch of their seemingly perfect holiday rental and say things like, 'This seems like a perfect place for us to unwind after all the work stress, honey. There's no way an axe murderer would be hiding anywhere around here.' Death is just minutes away, but everything seems normal.

Comedy appears glamorous to most onlookers, especially if they have never heard phrases like, 'I think we're going to hold the start by about fifteen minutes, see if anyone else shows up' or, 'The toilet's just down there; you need a bit of luck with the flush.' A comedian entertaining a room packed with people, enjoying their laughter and applause, is in a position that almost anyone would envy. The desire to hear about the bad moments, the times the laughter and applause *didn't* come, is a completely human and understandable product of that envy. If you have to watch someone radiating success, you at least want to feel they have suffered for it, overcome obstacles. You probably wouldn't go to see a film if the trailer went, 'RICH. HANDSOME. HE HAD THE WORLD AT HIS FEET. WHAT COULD GO WRONG? NOTHING, ACTUALLY. THIS CHRISTMAS, HEAR ABOUT A MAN WHO'S WAY BETTER THAN YOU.'

Yet while comedy as a career is widely seen as aspirational in the way professional football or rock stardom is, it also – as I've mentioned – fills people with a dread that those jobs do not. When a stranger asks, 'How do you get into something like that?' or, 'What made you do that, then?', it's in the same tone of faintly delighted horror as you might use if asking those questions to someone who took part in the Great Train Robbery.

It's a bit of a shame, then, that the answer to the first question is not, in most cases, very interesting. There's a well-known stand-up who got so bored with it coming up in interviews that he answered with a different lie every time and, if you google him, you'll find dozens of versions – for example, that he was a repairman and one time, when he couldn't fix someone's TV, he just stood in the corner of their room pretending to be all the different shows. We all know how easily a piece of nonsense fed to a journalist can crystallise into well-accepted fact on the internet. (My Wikipedia page says that I once built a dry-stone wall in an hour as part of one of my shows. I don't know who put it there and I certainly don't plan to change it back.)

The truth is that for most comedians, the journey into the business plays out much as it does for professionals in other fields: a period of apprenticeship, years of learning the trade, and then – with persistence, and some luck here and there – perhaps some degree of success. My journey, though, did start a little more dramatically than some, because (with an extended routine about the machismo of army recruitment adverts) I won the *Daily Telegraph* Open Mic competition at the Edinburgh Fringe in 2002. During the final of the competition, one of the comics slagged off the *Telegraph* relentlessly and I found myself wondering whether it was in the paper's best interests to sponsor it. Sure enough, they withdrew their sponsorship immediately afterwards, so I retained the trophy and am still, at forty-two, undefeated as the funniest young comedian around. The spotlight of attention from this win was short-lived, in the way the hype around these competitions always is, but it was enough to get me booked into a few comedy clubs – in London, then further afield. I would get the Megabus to Manchester and back, performing a handful of jokes in the middle of a twelve-hour round trip, arriving home at 6am. The discrepancy between travel time and actual stage time was often so great that – like all young comics – I often felt as if the motorway journeys *were* my job, and the brief moments of public speaking just a detail.

At the time of the Maidstone gig, I was about two years into this process, and the five-minute slots were becoming ten, occasionally even twenty. I was barely earning enough money to pay rent; one weekend my then partner and I were so skint we spent a couple of hours going through all the clothes in our wardrobe in case there were any forgotten banknotes in the pockets (there were not). When I went to visit my parents, I would wear an extra layer so that my mother didn't become worried that I wasn't feeding myself properly.

I'd graduated from a well-known university, and many of my peers were already on good starter salaries as paralegals or journalists or financial advisers. Not so many of them were waiting in the snow for the night bus home at 4am, and then moving seats twice during the journey because a stranger holding a cat in his lap kept wandering up the bus to sit next to them. Anyone witnessing a day in my life at this point would have been entitled to pose the next in our list of frequently asked questions: *why?*

There is a romantic answer, in my case, and a more uncomfortable one. We'll start with the former. At the age of twenty I went to the Edinburgh Fringe for the first of what is now, if we discount the pandemic, an unbroken streak of twenty-two Augusts. Until then I had seen almost no live comedy. It wasn't on TV anywhere near as much as it is now, and I never went to comedy clubs for much the same reason I never went to strip clubs: I wasn't exactly sure what went on there, but assumed it wasn't quite for me. (The average person's fear of being picked on, or called up to the stage, is so pronounced that you would probably have *more* success inviting them to a strip club.) Now, though, as part of a student play which fewer than a hundred people watched during the entire month, I found myself in the middle of the world's busiest and most intense arts festival: and a festival with a distinct slant towards comedy.

During the Fringe, almost everywhere you go in Edinburgh is a show venue. There are performances in churches, libraries, delicatessens. It wouldn't be a huge surprise to go to the zoo and find a penguin doing a ten-minute set on the frustratingly variable quality of fish at feeding time. Not only did I develop a mania for stand-up almost over-night, but for a month – both then, and the following August – I was in an environment where I could have as much of it as I could possibly consume. I wandered the city, gorging on comedy like a hungry traveller happening upon an all-you-can-eat buffet at a Toby Carvery (if this seems a very niche reference, wait till you've done a few hundred gigs).

As I watched my new heroes, these comedians – often thrillingly close-up, since Edinburgh specialises in squeez-ing performers and audience into dingy caves where people died of the plague in bygone times – I don't remember thinking, I could do that. But I definitely thought, I want to.

The main thing that enticed me about this (to me) un-familiar art form was, perhaps oddly, the same thing that makes it so daunting to others: the sheer solitude of it. The play I was performing in was something I had writ-ten and directed, with a cast of ten; there'd been a huge amount of rehearsal, discussion, cooperation. All this was fun, and rewarding, but also complicated and messy in the way large-scale collective efforts always are. These com-edians, by contrast, seemed just to be able to do what they wanted, whatever occurred to them. They weren't bound to a script (in reality some are, of course; part of their craft is in making you think otherwise). If something went wrong, if an audience member became a nuisance or they forgot their thread – the things you dread when you're in a play – they acknowledged it, made people laugh about it, made it into a positive. At its best, live comedy can take on a direction which not even the performer quite anticipated; it becomes an improvised expression of the pact between the person on stage and everyone who has come to see them. I'd never witnessed this sort of thing before, and I was hungry to try it for myself.

It wasn't just the autonomy which appealed to me, though: and here we come to the less rosy explanation for my ambition. It was also the fact that as a stand-up, it seemed to me, you would have so little responsibility to anyone but yourself.

I can't drive a car, ride a bike, open most food packaging or put up a shelf. Most days I get my trousers on, but it's by no means a given. I am bad at cooking, poor at almost all sports, undone by a range of parenting challenges. Many comics peddle this sort of 'What am I like?' shtick for laughs, but mine is not a shtick: I am the real deal. And I say that with no satisfaction. The difficulty I have with simple tasks was, and is, at the root of huge insecurities I have about myself and my ability to occupy a place in the world. (Admittedly, it did provide quite a lot of entertainment on *Taskmaster*.)

When I see professional competence of any kind – a bus driver not ploughing into a river, a waiter doing that trick where they pour the wine in an arc from a height of about two metres without a drop escaping – I feel two main things: envy of the skill and relief that I don't have to perform like that myself. That all I have to do is talk. That nobody is relying on me to get them to work or even pour them a drink. Of course, if a show doesn't go well, if I fail to give an audience the night they were hoping for, they will go away disappointed, and those are high stakes of a kind. But nobody is going to lose an important brain function as a result of that, as they might in Henry Marsh's place of work; nobody is even going to get wine spilled on a ballgown and complain to a manager. The only person who will really suffer, if I do my job badly, is me.

You can probably see both the allure of this – the independence it gives you, the self-reliance – and also the threat to the ego if it *were* to go wrong. But until this moment, it never had gone seriously wrong. I was inexperienced enough to think that perhaps it never would. I was about to learn an important lesson: that no comedian, no matter how talented, has that sort of exemption. That mortification, death on stage, is as inevitable as death itself.

The MC called my name, explaining that I was 'just going to do a short bit' in between a couple of the pros. You might think this would lower my status in the eyes of the audience, but the underdog tag had been useful to me in these situations so far; the lowered expectations meant I had a good chance of over-delivering. I walked on with the usual spring in my step, to a cautious smattering of applause.

I delivered my traditional first joke, a one-liner about 'sod's law', to near-silence. This had not happened before. Maybe I had stumbled over the wording or delivery; or maybe the finger of fate was just pointing at me that night. At once I felt my heart rate rise. There are circumstances in which this is good news – on a funfair ride, say, or recovering from cardiac arrest – but there are other circumstances in which it is extremely unwelcome, and near the top of that list we must place 'Trying to look assured in front of two hundred, mostly feral, people from Kent'. I delivered my second joke. Someone cleared their throat; in this atmosphere it sounded as loud as a firework. An alarm was ringing in my brain and I decided to skip straight to the best bit.

'Anyone seen those army adverts?' I asked, my voice very loud in my own ears. When a struggling comedian is on stage in a TV drama, there's nearly always a screech of feedback at this point. In real life, there is a far worse noise than a malfunctioning sound system, and that's the mutter and chair-scrape of a room gradually becoming restless. It flashed across my mind that Maidstone was a barracks town, and perhaps not the sort of place where a send-up of military pomposity would receive a standing ovation. It was a bit late to be thinking that, though, and besides: I had no other material.

'They all talk about how brave you have to be to join the army . . .' I began.

'Get off!' someone shouted from the back – this about ninety seconds after I got *on* – and the suggestion was the most popular thing that had happened during my brief tenure on the stage. Within another half-minute, the scene had spun wildly out of my control.

'Off! Off! Off!' yelled another one of my patrons. It gained popularity as rapidly as the 'Leave' campaign would, twelve years later, in the same part of the country. 'Off! Off!' chanted large sections of the room, as if heckling the whole of Europe across the water. I had become Donald Tusk – or that Belgian one with the more complicated, less pachyderm-like name.

Not much of this response was founded in genuine malice. The punters had already seen a couple of funny acts and had a well-known headliner still to come: why not enjoy something different in between? They meant me no real harm. They were just watching in the way casual viewers of a Formula One race watch two cars crash into one another. This was an event; a talking point. 'I went down the comedy club and this lad absolutely died a death' is an anecdote that will do well at work on Monday; 'I went down the comedy club and a young man showed quite a bit of resilience to come back from a difficult start' is not.

In the heat of the moment, though, I was feeling vulnerable up there in a way I never had before. What do real comedians do in this situation? I asked myself, feeling the prickling of sweat down my spine. They go on the offensive; they turn defence into attack. Find someone to pick on, I told myself: that's what a pro would do. I cast panicky looks at these strangers reeking of beer, at this gallery of people yelling at me to go home.

My eye was caught by the man who had started the 'off' chant. He had a head like the bowling ball you choose on your first turn before realising it's slightly too big and will wobble off to the side when you let it go. All right, I thought: let's go on the offensive. He had a red shirt. It wasn't much, but it would have to do.

'What are you shouting about, you red-shirted count?' I yelled, although the noun I used was somewhat ruder than 'count'. This was not a word I had ever said out loud before and it would be fair to say it didn't swing the pendulum of approval my way. If anything, the booing intensified.

Mentally, I was now pinned against the wall. I did the only thing I could: continue talking, just say anything under this canopy of abuse. I managed to last the full ten minutes. When I eventually said I was going to leave, the audience cheered for the first and only time. I walked off stage and the cheers went up a level. I tried not to meet the eyes of the other comedians. I heard the MC address the situation. 'Wow!' he said. '*That* was a death!' The audience laughed, gratefully. It was the first time I had heard the phrase in a club; the first time I'd seen a compère and a crowd bond over the humiliation of a man in front of their eyes. Everyone was in on it except me.

I gathered my belongings and started walking towards the exit. The show was still going on, but nonetheless people whispered and glanced as I hurried past them. Back out on the street, I followed signs to the station. The train was twenty-two minutes away from leaving. That was fine. That gave me time for a little cry.

It wasn't that I didn't know this could happen; that the whole enterprise was fraught with the potential for mortification. Even in my brief time in the game, I had seen plenty of people suffer on stage. The annals of open-mic comedy are littered with roadkill. In one of my early competition heats there was a girl who called herself the 'Mary Poppins Experience' and her performance consisted of her, dressed in full costume with umbrella, lip-synching extracts from the film *Mary Poppins* that were played in by a baffled technician. There weren't any jokes or, in fact, any live vocals at all. Quite understandably, nobody laughed and, after the results were read out, she left the pub without speaking to anyone, apparently unable to believe that she hadn't made it through to the next round.

I once saw an act get a lukewarm laugh for his opening gag, which wasn't so much a gag as him pointing out that his surname rhymed with the word 'toad'. Somehow this failed to raise the roof in the way he'd imagined. He snapped, 'I think I'll save the rest for a better audience,' and left the stage to boos within twenty-five seconds. I watched a 'new talent' contestant perform a series of jokes belonging word-for-word to Emo Philips, a unique and world-famous comic, and react angrily when it was put to him that this was plagiarism. And, furthermore, that he maybe should at least have changed the local references because it seemed a bit weird that he was a thirty-year-old from Peckham with stories that all took place in Los Angeles. After eighteen months as a newbie on the open-mic circuit I'd seen more people in tears than I would have if I'd spent that time as an apprentice funeral director.

But these characters were mostly misguided, I told myself. They were people who largely weren't cut out to be comedians and would work that out for themselves before too long. Indeed, many of them will be doing well in much more worthwhile and less emotionally punishing fields than comedy by now (I do sometimes wonder about the 'Mary Poppins' lady; I expect she's a project manager, or something). On some level, and with a young man's arrogance, I believed that I was a different species. That I'd stumbled upon something I could do with my life which I was perfectly adapted to, which would remove my inferiority complex.

None of these hopes had been wiped out by a single disastrous gig, of course, but that *was* how it felt as I stared out of the window of the train taking me back to the flat I could only just pay the rent on. For a start, filling the diary with work as a young comedian is a matter of momentum, a game of snakes and ladders. The better your gigs go, the better your odds of being booked for more, over the dozens of other comedians vying for the same opportunity. The reverse, naturally, also feels true: slither down a snake like the one lying in wait in Maidstone, and you've undone the good work of the last ten ladders. I told myself that word of my failure would already have reached not just the woman who booked me for the show and who would now regard me as a liability, but all other bookers of comedy shows. By the time I got off the train and walked, chastened, to catch a bus I could barely afford to board, I'd more or less convinced myself that my bad-gig news was being flashed up on the giant billboards in Times Square and that a 'DO NOT ADMIT' poster, bearing my face, had already been pasted up in every venue in the country.

Of course, a few days' recovery took at least some of the edges off these spiralling fantasies; by the following weekend I'd downgraded the newsflashes from Times Square to Piccadilly Circus, and 'DO NOT ADMIT' to 'ONLY BOOK IF NO OTHER COMEDIAN IS AVAILABLE'. I went back into battle. Walking on stage for the first time since the humiliation was considerably more nerve-racking than the very first time had been: the scale of possible disaster, the distance there was to fall, was now far more apparent to me than it had been before. Everything seemed to be all right, though. The army advert spoof hit its target; the audience in general were appreciative; I did not, at any point, break into a cold sweat or yell the c-word at anybody. Fairly quickly, the misery of April 9th came to occupy what seemed a useful place in my consciousness. The gig served as a battle scar; it was a testament to survival. Nothing, I told myself, would ever be quite as painful as that again.

In one sense it was true. I was never again to die on stage quite as fully and excruciatingly as on that night – at least, not yet. On the scale of sorrow that was ahead of me, though, Maidstone had been little more than a warm-up.

Mortification is written right into the DNA of my life and career stories. And perhaps I should have known that even by the age of twenty-four, because it had started happening well before then.

2

WE DON'T REALLY KNOW
WHAT WE'RE DOING

Christmas carol service, Shirehampton, Bristol, 1991. I'm about to sing a solo, everyone is looking at me, my parents and their friends are in the audience, the church is holding its breath. And I know, deep down, that everything is on the verge of going badly, badly wrong.

This is a common sort of scene in anxiety dreams – you've got an unusually restful subconscious if you haven't dreamed about taking the stage in a play without knowing what your lines are or showing up to an exam to find that you revised the wrong subject and also you're naked and the cast of *Friends* are pointing at you. But the carol concert is no dream. It is as real as the strange blue robe and white collar I'm wearing; as real as the vicar, Rev. Daniels, a powerful speaker who, unfortunately, looks a bit poorly under the festive lights because the Lord did not decide to give him a working pair of kidneys.

I watch the other singers, one at a time, dispatch their solos to applause. To draw an anachronistic comparison, because we're a decade away from the craze of TV singing shows, I imagine it's a similar feeling to the one *X Factor* contestants might get as they hear all the previous singers wowing the judges and think, Well, *someone's* going to get annihilated or it's not much of a show.

But my rising fear is not purely based on superstition or jealousy. It's also not just the nerves of the big occasion. If I were the sort to bottle it when things got tense, would I have been made vice-captain of the school chess team? (Admittedly, I'm not completely sure why we had a vice-captain; it isn't a sport where you get a lot of injuries.) Even aged eleven, I've got plenty of form with Christmas concerts. I've pulled off Bible readings before – in fact, that's how I learned the word 'fornication' aged eight, to the surprise of my parents. The previous year I not only read a humorous poem about Mary and Joseph's trip to Bethlehem, but a humorous poem *of my own creation*, with a couple of pretty successful gags about what it's like being pregnant on a donkey. This was not the kind of material many ten-year-old poets were doing at the time. You'll be taking your hat off to me if you've also ever tried getting laughs out of the grandparent-heavy Christmas concert crowd.

Yes, I'm one of the big hitters round here; I'm one of the names you pay your £1.50 to see. The problem for me is that the run-up to this year's gig hasn't exactly been smooth. Things haven't been going *badly* in rehearsals but, secretly, I know that they haven't been going too well, either. The fact is that, ever since the solos were assigned in October, my body has started to undergo some of the changes you read about in the books you wish your parents hadn't given you, and which you learn about at school and nobody can look anyone else in the face (there's a classmate I still haven't spoken to properly since one of those biology lessons, and it's been twenty-nine years now).

My voice – there's no escaping it – has been among the casualties. It isn't reaching quite the range it used to. I've tried to put the change down to a couple of off-days – any chorister will confirm that you sometimes get duff moments when singing at the highest level – but in my guts, now, I know that, unless something remarkable happens in the next ten minutes to reverse the onset of adolescence, I'm not going to get all the way up to the top notes in front of all these people.

The 'O Christmas Tree' solo has come at a tough time. My notion of being a world-renowned singer like Aled Jones is about to go the same way as my previous dreams of being a professional footballer, publishing a fiction series by the time I was ten, and being the first kid to edit a national newspaper. The dream is about to die.

All of us can look back on dreams and ambitions we've had earlier in life and concede that they were always unlikely to come off. There are not enough job opportunities for ballet dancers, TV presenters or monarchs to accommo-date any but the most talented, fortunate and/or royal. If your mum is like most people's, she'll have at least one recollection of an amusingly far-fetched thing that you once wanted to do when you grew up. She might even have kept a scrapbook in which you've drawn a picture of yourself scoring a goal for England, which comes out every Christmas, at your wedding and at any point when there are more than four people in the house. You have to laugh sportingly and agree, 'Ha, yes, I did imagine myself attaining international sports honours one day, when in fact ultimately I only played once for the school's B team, and that was as a substitute and *that* was because Jamie Crawford got his ear stuck in the school gate while yelling at a friend.' Or maybe you have a parent who kept the pipe dream alive long after you snuffed it out yourself and likes to imply that pursuing the unattainable would have been better than whatever you did end up devoting your time on earth to. (You know, the sort of parent who turns up at the ceremony to collect your Nobel Prize, awarded for helping to prevent a civil war, and says, 'I always thought you would have been a good dentist. Knew everything about teeth, didn't he, Colin?')

The gap between what we think life is going to be like, and the way it turns out, is not only a perennial round-the-dinner-table subject, but also tells us some-thing fundamental about our relationship with our own destinies, which is – to be blunt about it – that we know jack shit. There's a bit in a Chaucer poem where he says that, in trying to find our path through life, we are all a bit like a man coming home hammered and trying to remember which house is his. Or to use a slightly more recent reference, Søren Kierkegaard famously wrote, 'Life can only be understood backwards, but must be lived forwards.' (Don't worry, that's probably the last of the quotations, because those are pretty much the only two things I can remember from the three years of my English degree.) The Kierkegaard one, in particular, has always appealed to me, because it's so obviously true that even yesterday you made decisions which you might have avoided with today's knowledge. We are always one step behind ourselves, always beginning sentences with 'If I'd only known . . .'

We attribute this short-sightedness or general folly to our younger versions, never to our current selves. We find it easy to laugh at our tatty old 'When I Grow Up' essays, because we've got childish handwriting and have drawn our own head the same size as a horse; we can see it was rash to drop out of an archaeology degree and retrain as a catwalk model or vice versa, but we never seem to think: This means that, a few years from now, what I'm doing *today* might seem ridiculous, or at least, it won't seem to have been worth getting as anxiously consumed by it as I am right now.

We can look back at old emails marked 'MORE URGENT THAN ANYTHING ELSE THAT AWAITS

YOU IN LIFE' and struggle to remember what they even refer to; we can come across an old to-do list on which one item has been underlined so many times the pen went through the paper and roll our eyes at what a waste of time that briefly burning issue turned out to be. But that doesn't prevent us from beating ourselves up over today's task that doesn't get done or being devastated when a dating app turns out not to be the magical solution to loneliness it claimed to be. If you could just see your current worries through the amused eyes of future you, you'd realise they're an awful lot smaller than they look; so few of the things we plan are anywhere near guaranteed to happen. 'Most things don't happen.' Remember that: we'll come back to it.

Why do we all rush headlong through life like this, fixated with concerns that aren't as crucial as we think, reassessing with hindsight, and then crashing straight on to make the same mistakes? I think it's to do with the way we grow up. Not necessarily because of specific parents or teachers. Just because the whole world is filling us with ideas which will, at some point, send us mad. *How* mad, though, depends on how much importance we place on prizes, attention and glory. This was a problem for me even before I set my heart on being the world's favourite boy soprano. And child publishing sensation. And first under-twelve editor of a national newspaper. Yes: in terms of healthy perspectives, I think I've always been that stick-figure with a head the size of a horse.

★

I've always put a disproportionate amount of pressure on myself to achieve. It's hard to say why this is. It certainly doesn't reflect the attitudes of my parents, who were never the pushy, hot-housing types. They created an atmosphere in which my three siblings and I felt, more or less, free to try and accomplish whatever we wanted, but not under enormous pressure to do so. I didn't come from a showbiz dynasty or a household with a massive onus to carry on a tradition.

My dad is a chemistry teacher and he never made me feel like I had to become one of the millionaire celebrity chemistry teachers. In fact, maybe my parents were so easy-going that they held us back from greatness. If only they'd loved us enough to make us hit a tennis ball against the garage door with a saucepan for fourteen hours a day, who knows how many Wimbledons we would have won between us? As it is, I'm embarrassed to say not one of us has won a grand slam title. My mum had to stop chatting to Venus and Serena's dad over the fence in the end because it all got too much.

My brother and sisters used this latitude to do impressively off-the-wall things: working for a sports organisation that represents marginalised or unrecognised states and running a charity for impoverished families in Moldova . . . all very laudable, but I – the first-born – wanted the headlines. At junior school, despite being reasonably high up in the academic pecking order, I seemingly couldn't get enough validation and attention. When my friend Erin won a painting competition and had her work exhibited in our local library, I claimed that I'd also won in a different category but the library had lost my work and I had been ordered not to tell anyone. When writing an English exercise about my family, I decided that my lineage wasn't dramatic enough and claimed that my grandfather was from Fiji and had represented Fiji at rugby (supplying as proof an illustration of my fictitious relative – a black man – scoring a try) – a claim that began to unravel at the next parents' evening when my teacher addressed my baffled mum with the words, 'How fascinating about your father.' When word got around that the dad of a kid called James had been seriously ill in hospital and he got a special mention in assembly, I tried to start a playground rumour that mine had died in a car crash and come back to life. This fantasising (being sympathetic) or utter mendacity (more accurate) could be seen as the early signs of someone who was almost certain to become a storyteller by trade. A less charitable reading would be that it was also an indication of someone whose desperation to be in the spotlight would probably lead him to write off enormous swathes of dignity in the interest of chasing a hit.

I was never going to be much use at sport, but in the fields of writing and performance – where I had a bit of early encouragement – my ambitions knew no bounds. Nor should they, as far as I was concerned, because an intimidating precedent had been set. There was a celebrity schoolgirl called Jayne Fisher who had published a whole series of books about a group of anthropomorphised vegetables called the Garden Gang (Mark Marrow was one of them; I was a bit disappointed not to get a more mainstream veg). These were real, actual books, available as Ladybird hardbacks, with the author's photo on the back, easily found in schools and libraries, *and they had been written by a nine-year-old*. It was exciting to know that this could be done, but the knowledge was also terrible. I felt I would be underachieving if I didn't have a canon of work in print before I hit double figures.

I searched desperately and in vain for the hook that would persuade a publisher to put me on the same footing as Jayne Fisher – who I assumed lived in a mansion with her own bouncy castle and could have as many Fruit Pastilles as she wanted, rather than having to wait for Sunday like all the non-published losers like me. My longest-running series was called *Mark and Heather* and featured me alongside a girl I'd got to know when we lived in Canada for a year, at the age of four. Even these very early works show signs of massive insecurity alongside the ego that makes any child cast themselves as the hero of a story. In *Mark and Heather Back in Time*, for example, things start fairly conservatively as the duo take in the 1966 World Cup final (then only twenty years in the past), but then they skip all the way back to the Garden of Eden. On seeing the dawn of humanity, Mark faints, has to be revived and abandons the expedition. You can see why this timid young man might not have struck the literary world as the hero a generation was waiting for and, although I insisted that my efforts were sent out to publishers, you can also see in retrospect that Chris and Margaret Watson were right to do as they did, which was instead to stash these books in the attic and wait for them to become good fodder for an autobiography. My tenth birthday came and went. I didn't see why people thought it was worth celebrating. You wouldn't have balloons and cake at a funeral.

Not long after this I set my sights on journalism, noting that every weekend when the *Sunday Express* landed on the kitchen table, my parents – especially my father – were transfixed. Perhaps the papers were the way to reach an audience, I started to think. It didn't seem likely that I could manage the commute to Fleet Street every day while also holding down a place in a Year 5 class at school and, once more, I was forced to go DIY. I began writing and publishing my own paper. By now my operation was a bit slicker; I had successfully sourced a stapler. As with *Mark and Heather*, there remain several copies of this respected news source still in existence and their pages reveal an editor experimenting with content to try to draw in a readership. There are articles on Watson family household matters and sport but also an attempt to reach an older audience: there's an advertisement for a made-up pub with the 'best beer' and a crossword competition in which the top prize was £100,000 and a lorry (I don't remember how I came by these items to give away, but the *Daily Blah* must have had some major sponsorship).

In this period, I also wrote to *Jim'll Fix It*, which people my sort of age will remember as a massively effective shortcut to getting your dreams achieved, except that Jim never waved his magic wand over my request, 'Please fix it for me to have a career as a journalist.' Perhaps understandably the producers must have decided against making a feature-length, twenty-year episode that followed me through journalism college and a series of local papers until I got a column. (If you were born in the nineties or later, by the way, and you have to google *Jim'll Fix It*, you will come across some alarming information about this man, and – yes – suffice to say that if I *had* ended up with a photo of Jimmy Savile presenting me with a medal, it's unlikely it would still be up on my mum's pinboard.)

My Charles Foster Kane ambitions started to fade when I realised there was a flaw in my strategy: it was extremely hard for me to get scoops. Living in suburban Bristol, being seven years too young to hold a driving licence and not being in touch with anyone who lived more than half a mile away, all took their toll on my ability to keep my finger on the world's pulse. The only way I could find stories to report on was by looking at the headlines of existing newspapers – normally in Londis when my mum popped in for groceries – that I would then rehash for my parents to read.

If I could have looked forward in time, to the age of social media, and seen how much journalism would consist of people reporting what other people had already said, perhaps I wouldn't have relinquished my plans quite so quickly. But my heart wasn't quite in it anymore, and there was also the financial blow of having to give my dad a hundred grand and buy him a lorry once he'd completed the crossword. The *Daily Blah* became an early casualty of the print media decline which would eventually claim the *News of the World* too, and for much the same reason: there wasn't any point in its existence.

And so, I started to get interested in the other obvious route to stardom: choirboy. To be clear, it wasn't all about the bright lights. I was keen to please my mum, who was a churchgoer at the time, and I was in two minds whether there was a God but, if so, it definitely seemed worth pleasing him, too. There were also almost no rivals for the position in my area. The choir, when I joined it, consisted of just three male voices: me, with my flute-like tones, a big middle-aged man called Jon who sang in a bass so deep that the only members of the congregation who could hear him were buried in the churchyard out back, and a teenager named Kai whose voice was somewhere in the middle and whose form was variable. One Christmas Eve he turned up drunk and, as we did our joyful procession around the church, he lurched away to be sick on an altar candle. I say 'procession', but it's a stretch to describe it as such when there are only three people; once you're down to two, it's really just a walk.

I began to enjoy having the plucky-underdog status of life in an almost non-existent choir, not to mention the enormous wages. You didn't get paid for singing in a regular church service, but if there was a wedding on a Saturday you would get three quid. Sometimes our trio would team up with other local choirs – as happened with the carol concert – and we would go out as an emergency nuptials taskforce, like a formally dressed A-Team. On one memorable day we did a hat-trick of weddings in an afternoon, coming away nine pounds richer, which in those days could buy you a house. I had hit paydirt at last. Not Jayne Fisher money, no, but we were getting somewhere.

Once again, though, rather than be content with the extremely localised kudos attached to being virtually the only singer in town, I allowed myself to dream of bigger things. When we went to those weddings at other churches, I would find myself singing extra hard and doing proper choirboy expressions like they did on *Songs of Praise*, in case there were any choir scouts prowling around who might snap me up and put me on a bigger stage. Like, for example, the ones Aled Jones was on. He wasn't just 'the equivalent of a pop star': he had actually been a pop star as recently as Christmas 1985, when his cover version of 'Walking in the Air', from the film *The Snowman*, was No. 5 in the charts, above Wham! and Bruce Springsteen. (Most people of my generation still believe that Jones sang the earlier version in the film itself and those of us who know the truth can mostly still remember where we were when we found out.)

The lesson of Jones's smash hit seemed clear: a single flex of the tonsils in the right church could make you a bigger star than George Michael. This idea was still somewhere in the back of my mind on the day I humbly accepted the commission to sing the 'O Christmas Tree' solo. Maybe the vestige of it was still there, even as I stood waiting for my turn.

I went up to the microphone. I could see my mum and the assorted neurosurgeons she had corralled into attendance. (My mother, I should clarify, was a medical secretary to a neurosurgeon; she didn't just go through the phone book calling doctors when she needed a crowd.) Even my dad was there: a man profoundly uninterested in matters of faith, who – when I asked at the age of seven whether my hamster was likely to go to heaven – avoided the traditional 'No one really knows' sidestep and said, 'I shouldn't have thought so, no.' This was a big moment in my singing career and in the expectant silence I could hear my own ragged breaths.

I launched in. You'll be familiar with the carol, often known as 'O Tannenbaum', which is the German original. I don't think I'm exaggerating when I say it's one of the most famous songs ever addressed directly to a tree and, in a carol service, it can be a welcome change from the otherwise fairly pointed emphasis on the miraculous-baby-pointed-out-by-a-star, his parents' difficulty sourcing accommodation and so on.

I made it through the first couple of lines, but there was no getting away from it: my voice was straining to reach the key the choirmaster was playing. I started to wonder whether it had been a mistake to beat him at table-tennis.

At 'The sight of thee at Christmastide/ Spreads hope and gladness far and wide', my vocal chords ran out of gas. No sound came out whatsoever. For about ten seconds – the longest of my life at that point, even including the intense chess battle against Monks Park primary – there was no singing at all. It was what they call, on the radio, 'dead air'.

I groped around for the end of the verse and eventually managed to force out some vaguely recognisable sounds, shuffling back to join the choir in which, I felt, my time had come to a brutally sudden end. A couple of people muttered, 'Well done,' but most of what their faces communicated was sympathy. In the sputtering of my vocal range, some of the slightly younger ones had perhaps seen a glimpse of Christmas future.

Afterwards, Mum was as partisan as ever. She was then – and is now – the most devoted fan a boy could have; if I drowned during a swimming gala she'd still maintain I was the real winner. She said my performance had been beautiful; had given her, in her own words, 'goosebumps all down my arms'. I still get goosebumps when I think of it, too. But not for the same reasons.

Nobody ever said anything unkind about my solo and nobody from school had been present; 'Watson's voice broke' never became a hot piece of playground gossip. But the damage was done in my mind. I knew that when my voice did set up a new base camp, it would be at a much lower altitude. I wouldn't be the next Aled Jones. I'd just be another guy plodding through the unglamorous bits of the harmonies, one of those banned from the first 'O come, let us adore Him' of 'O Come, All Ye Faithful' and reduced to bellowing the last one. I'd make the sad journey from the front choir stall to the rear and take my place next to Jon, the bass, sliding further and further down the octaves.

I'd committed no crime, other than to be caught between the ages of eleven and twelve at the wrong time. And that, it's fair to say, happens to every young man. But like everything else I'm going to recount, the mortification felt like mine alone. It felt like failure.

I doubt you had quite as many delusions as I did, at the age of ten, about the likelihood of becoming a globally renowned provider of turnip-based fiction or choral work. But you'll be familiar with the sinking feeling you get when you realise something you wanted is out of reach. It doesn't have to be as overblown an ambition as to play on centre court, star in a film or succeed in transferring a SIM card from one phone to another. Almost all of us, at some point, hear of someone else's achievement and think, I should have done that by now.

The reason for this lies in the way we are conditioned to approach life, which is basically never to see it as a thing to be enjoyed in the present, but always as a set of possible futures. You'll have read the phrase, 'Live in the moment' many times – often on Facebook, accompanied by a graphic of someone white-water rafting or being half killed at Alton Towers. As with a lot of useful tips, it's come to seem a bit empty. But beneath the social media sentiment and the yoga-retreat associations, 'living in the moment' is a pretty essential rule.

It doesn't mean that you should wring the maximum drama out of every hour of each day, as social media can often imply. It just means that it's crucial to feel alive, notice what is happening, enjoy as much as you can of what is actually around you *now*, this minute, rather than letting your attention wander endlessly towards what better thing might come next. (To give you an example, you could start by committing fully to enjoying this book now, rather than looking forward to the thriller set in a zoo which you've got lined up ready to go next. I'm sure it's great and everything but give me a chance, will you?)

Our psyches are wired to strike out exhaustingly in the direction of the future because, from day one, everyone else is doing that for us. Almost from the moment after birth we're laid on a table to be weighed and measured, somebody not too far away is yelling, 'WHAT ARE YOU GOING TO BE WHEN YOU GROW UP? COULD BE A BUILDER WITH THOSE ARMS?'

As you'll know if you've had children or younger siblings, almost anything a kid does is taken as proof of what might be to come, rather than something to be enjoyed for its own sake. He's smashing the shit out of that xylophone some maniac bought him for Christmas? He'll be in a band. She's managed to get hold of a biscuit even though you could swear you shut the tin and put it on a high shelf? She's going to be a secret agent. This sort of speculation intensifies once we get to school, especially in the current climate in which the government places ruthless emphasis on testing and grading, filtering children down towards the appropriate pools of the labour market, when they're barely old enough to write the word 'job'. By the time you're about fourteen there will be enormous pressure to know everything you're going to do for the next fifty years. I remember my brother, around that age, being asked by a well-meaning relative, 'So, do you know what university you're going to go to yet?'

'The University of Crime,' said Paul, rising from Sunday lunch and leaving the table in an uneasy silence that was only broken when our mum offered the gravy round for a second time.

All of us do it, often unconsciously, because talking about unknowns, about possible worlds, is fun and exciting – more so than the mundane realities we occupy. Someone gets a promotion at work? At least one commenter will ask, 'So what's the next step up after this? World domination?' In an interview about a comedy show, regardless of how much work I might have put in and how proud I am of the results, I'll always be asked, 'And what are you doing next?' – making me feel that the thing I have just finished is already passé or dull to talk about, that it's time to try again in the hope of making something which really *is* the business. I imagine when Neil Armstrong and his team returned from the moon, it was only about half an hour before someone asked what other projects were in the pipeline.

These questions are almost always well-meaning and posed in a spirit of excitement and genuine enthusiasm for all the possible paths that might open up in the future. But the more of these paths that are illuminated, the more opportunities you have to feel that you've missed by not taking them all – even though you can't possibly try everything. All of us are aware of the poem about the 'road less travelled' making all the difference. But there are very rarely just 'two paths in a wood'. Life in the modern world is more like one of those dystopian superhighways seen on short films about how cars are choking the planet. There are about twenty lanes to choose from and, as soon as you choose the 'less travelled' one, another one becomes still *less* well travelled and you wish you'd headed down that one instead.

Some paths aren't even visible. Without wanting to sound like a cryptic old hermit you're encountering somewhere in the Andes who makes you answer three questions before giving you directions up the mountain: sometimes you have to have walked the path *before* you can see it behind you. Far more often than we like to admit, we don't really know what we're doing. We don't know where we're going. The most concrete plans we make for our lives are often less important than what happens *to* us and how we respond. And one of the key steps to happiness is to accept that that's fine. It's OK that one of the steps to happiness is that there might not *be* steps to happiness.

There I go again with the mystic hermit stuff. I'm dangerously close to leading a guided meditation here.

This acceptance goes against all the instincts and conditioning that urge us to identify what we want in life and march relentlessly towards it until it becomes ours. We're easily daunted by people who seem to have it all mapped out and wish we were more like them.

One of the things that attracted me to my university of choice was that it had a reputation for opportunities in performing and writing, the things I was still reasonably sure I wanted to devote my life to. Since 'O Christmas Tree' and its fallout I'd made slow progress towards a career in the arts. The main roles I'd taken in my life at that point were a piece of seaweed in *The Little Mermaid* (which involved wearing tights) and a really, really old man with not much to say in *The Crucible* (which involved wearing tights *and* having talcum powder in my hair). To summarise, I'd had a lot of difficulty making that all-important transition to parts where you could wear trousers, even in the limited field of secondary-school drama. I'd made a name for myself writing rugby reports for the school noticeboard, and got a holiday job working on a listings magazine. The magazine supported itself with 'paid editorial' – pieces which serve as ads, but are meant to look like real articles – so a lot of my role was to write sentences like: 'You might think the good old-fashioned fireplace has gone out of fashion. But step into Grate Expectations on the Gloucester Road and you'll need to think again.' I'd won a public speaking competition and represented my school at debating (we lost). That was it so far, more or less: powder in hair, home furnishings journalism.

Would it be enough to hit the ground running at university? The answer will not surprise you. There was once an episode of *The Apprentice* in which Claude Littner, a sort of pantomime villain whose job is to psychologically unsettle the candidates, snapped at someone: 'You're not a big fish. You're not *even* a fish.' That sums up what felt like my status in the huge new pond I'd been dropped into. Many of the people I met, especially those with an eye on the arts, were full of talk about long-term-goals and five-year-plans, some of which seemed to be *already underway*. I met fellow freshers who had spent a summer working at *The Times*, who had directed shows at the Fringe (which I'd never been to, at this stage), who already somehow had a theatrical and film agent. I'd come to uni thinking that these were the sort of doors that three years of effort and enterprise might open for me and now I was running into people who casually said things like, 'That door? Oh, yes, it's not there anymore; I opened it, walked through it, took it off its hinges and it's now hanging in my flat as a trophy next to the Day of the Dead skulls from my gap year.'

That was the other thing: almost everyone apart from me seemed to have spent the year travelling, enriching their cultural lives and ploughing through the recommended reading – which, for English literature, was such a forbidding list that it was an achievement even to finish it, let alone the books themselves. On my very first evening, at the getting-to-know-you dinner, I found myself between two people who had both spent gap years not just in Mexico, not even just in the same province of Mexico, but what started to sound like the same street. As they flung Spanish slang back and forth across my sad little bread roll, I experienced the first taste of a feeling which would haunt me at university: the feeling of having missed a meeting at which everyone else was given a crucial piece of information. Sometimes, to be fair, it *was* because I'd missed a meeting at which everyone else was given a crucial piece of information. But in a more general way it was impostor syndrome. The belief that you don't belong in a job or position, don't deserve the praise you've received or the authority you have. That you are going to get found out. That at any minute someone might rip the mask off your face.

I felt endlessly behind in the race to hit the checkpoints you were apparently meant to hit during what are often called the 'best years of your life'. It's particularly hard to appreciate the time you spend at university in the moment precisely because people are excited about what's around the corner for you and won't stop telling you so. If you're reading this with college or university or anything like that ahead of you, I'm not saying that people are necessarily wrong when they tell you you're going to form amazing memories, make crucial friendships, set yourself up well for the future and so on. Just don't allow those possibilities to turn into pressures and don't be so anxiously looking ahead for them that you forget to look up and enjoy what's going on right now.

What allowed me to turn the corner – and it wasn't until my final year – was that I released myself from those pressures by doing something purely for fun. My friend Benet and I wrote some sketches and booked a tiny theatre almost on a whim. It went down pretty well with an audience of people drawn exclusively from our own college, but it was slightly hard to see how our takedowns of the layout of my accommodation in FF staircase, or the way a particular tutor stood when he was queuing for dinner, would take us to the big league.

And yet, indirectly, it *did* help me to get to the place I'm writing from today. A touring comedy show, with three professional club comedians, came to our college. Three days before the event, a panicking entertainment organiser, or 'ents officer', as we unfortunately used to call them, told me that one of the comedians had pulled out through illness: something which I took at face value at the time, though twenty years on, and slightly more jaded, it seems likely the 'illness' was a severe case of 'being offered a more lucrative gig that is not in a students' union'. The officer wondered whether I wanted to take the vacant slot on the line-up. It ought to have been a terrifying prospect, but for some reason it seemed fun, instead. I knew that if I was brought on as someone who had volunteered to save the day, I would have the audience onside pretty quickly. And, once more, there was the advantage of being on home turf that I had over the real comedians, who were unlikely to have material about the amount of time it took to walk to the economics lecture building. Also, it was *not* technically volunteering: the event organiser offered me thirty pounds, which – measured in the only meaningful metric of the day – was a lot of pasta and Mars bars.

I had no idea how to write stand-up or how to put a set together and, as I've said, I had really only ever seen a handful of comedians; but all this was almost an advantage. I wasn't weighed down, as young comedians sometimes can be, by the knowledge of all the great people who were already out there doing the same thing or by the temptation to mimic what they were doing. I wrote some jokes, memorised them and walked on to the stage. No record of the show exists – not even a clip on someone's phone because in those days a phone was the size of a scanner – and I couldn't be more grateful for that. There's little doubt I would think it was dreadful if I saw it now. But on its own terms, it was a success. People I'd barely spoken to in two-and-a-bit years were asking when I was going to do more shows (a question I couldn't really answer, because my only tactic for getting booked was waiting for comedians to pull out of shows and saying, 'Here I am!'). And for once they were right to talk about the future because, more by good fortune than anything else, I had stumbled across mine.

If you're about my age, you might well have played a board game called Game of Life, which does indeed put you in a car, making your way in one direction around a board collecting progressively more valuable properties and family members. (I played the modern version with my children recently, and very little has changed, except these days you can go on holiday to Dubai and get a job as a music producer.)

But life, as I've already said, is not a game, and nor is it something you approach with a roadmap. If it *were* a game and that game were football, the goals wouldn't be standing there at opposite ends of the pitch with people cheering you on as you got closer to them. You'd just be asked to boot the ball around random spots and only when the game was over would someone tell you what the score was. (Some would say this is indeed where we're headed with VAR, but that is a subject for a quite different book.)

Goals are worth having, yes. Some sort of ambition is essential, or you'd never progress beyond lying in bed eating crisps (although if your ambition is to be a bed-and-crisps influencer and you're good-looking enough, these days you can probably monetise that). But an ambition – whether it's to be Aled Jones or just to be slightly fitter next month than you are today – needs to be a positive, something that drives you pleasurably on, rather than a stick to beat yourself with if things don't play out the way you planned. You won't meet all goals – but you don't have to, because the things you do instead will turn out to have had far more value.

I could have found a way into comedy by hearing that a show was coming to our college, actively asking if I could get a five-minute spot, studying the routines of famous comedians, trying to tailor my act to be more like theirs, asking the other acts on the bill how they got where they were, perhaps writing to their agents and so on. Some of these things I did go on to do, in fact, when I began to understand that standing in a room talking nonsense was something I might be able to make into a job. But it bears repeating that one of the most important steps I ever took on my path in life was one I took more or less in the dark. The path wasn't marked, and I hadn't even been trying to find it.

Sometimes, life is not about chasing down your targets, no matter what the motivational experts tell you. Sometimes the chances you want in life will come looking for you and you just need to spot them. When some people describe how they, and these are very pronounced inverted commas, 'made it', they'll often make it sound as if they planned every detail in advance. And maybe, in their memory, that's how it was. But that's because our minds tend to edit out the times we improvised, relied on other people, or got lucky. Those parts are less satisfying as a story, after all, and we're constantly telling ourselves stories. They're just not always accurate.

If you ever find yourself thinking that an avenue has been closed forever, that there's something you wanted in life that you've irretrievably blown your chances of getting, try to recall something from your past that beat you up as much as my aborted Christmas solo and think how little it turned out to matter in the end. Life, remember, can only be understood backwards. And sometimes we don't even get that bit right.

3

PEOPLE SEEMED INTERESTED

I've talked a fair bit, in these opening chapters, about the idea that success and failure largely come down to circumstances beyond your control. This is something I firmly believe, but I don't mean to imply that there's no point putting effort into projects and pursuing what you most want in life. It's just worth being mindful of the fact that life won't always reward those efforts.

Maidstone is a little way behind us; I am making slow progress up the ladder of live comedy. And something huge has happened: I've had a novel published. I'd written it as a recent graduate, doing sixteen-hour days and longer, sometimes: staring out of the window at the orange streetlights at 4am as I closed the barely serviceable laptop I was writing on, then getting up at 10am and starting again. It had been a struggle to find an agent to offer it to publishers; dozens of polite, regretful emails, until I fell on the mercy of an agent called Francis, who only glanced at my manuscript because a friend of mine was doing work experience in his office and did me what proved to be a huge favour. Even then, Francis was snubbed by what seemed like every publisher in the universe when he sent it out. Under his tutelage, though, I did a massive rewrite of the book and came back six months later with a different version. This time, someone said yes.

Here we are. Fifteen years after the *Mark and Heather* books failed to find a foothold, a lifelong ambition is fulfilled. Surely those childhood books will be hoovered up by the publisher too, when the massive success of this novel – *Bullet Points* – encourages them to acquire my entire back catalogue. Where are you now, Jayne Fisher? Talking sweetcorn not quite such an easy sell when you're in your early thirties, huh?

Admittedly, the hardback edition of the novel hasn't set the world alight. It's fair to say, in fact, that it has left the world at exactly the same temperature. But that's fine, according to the publishers: the paperback is what it's really all about. This is where it's going to get exciting. There's been a lunch to celebrate the release in the Oxo Tower, on London's South Bank, which – to someone of my suburban background – feels as if the publishers have gone to New York to rent the Empire State Building with Jay Gatsby as host.

Now we're on our way to a book event, in Ayr, the west of Scotland. I'm on the train with the publishers' PR, Chloe – Scottish herself, knows the territory, keeps mentioning how pretty it is up there, how friendly everyone is going to be. I'm sure she's right. Scotland isn't enormous, I tell myself; all the people who live there must be in reasonably regular touch.

Even the idea of travelling with a one-person entourage is, of course, a bizarre novelty. Chloe is not much older than me and she takes her duty of care pretty seriously. Before we'd got on the train at King's Cross, she brought 20p out of her purse for admission to the toilet, then produced another 20p and gave it to me. Is this the level of personal attention I should now expect? Will I soon be able to stop carrying money altogether, like the Queen?

The numbers expected for this event, many miles from home, are — according to Chloe — 'between fifty and a hundred, but it could be more'. It's impossible to be sure, because it's free; the bookshop has been giving out invitations with every book they've sold. A slightly older and more jaded version of your narrator might have raised an eyebrow at this. These days I know that an audience of fifty is a lot for a book event. To be completely honest, for a first-time novelist nobody has heard of, in a town in which he knows nobody, on a midweek night, twenty wouldn't be bad. So it was optimistic to say that it 'could be more' than one hundred. There's not been an event since Woodstock at which more people showed up than the organisers had bargained for. That's just what we're all like. Everyone reading this has had the experience of booking an event, maybe even paying good money for tickets, having it in the diary for ages and, as the date falls, thinking, Ooh, I tell you what would be great – not bothering to go to that thing tonight. Taking a leaflet a few weeks ahead of a talk and saying, 'Thanks, I might try and get along to that,' is a very different proposition to spending a fortnight with an electronic counter ticking down in your kitchen: 'JUST 134 HOURS TILL WATSON!' Particularly when – to stress again – there was absolutely no reason for anyone living within a hundred miles of the bookshop to know who I was.

But I, the twenty-four-year-old Mark Watson, didn't know how anything works in publishing. At the time, I was happy to wallow in the optimism of people I presumed were far better informed. I had been on *BBC Breakfast* to talk about the book (with LeAnn Rimes of 'Can't Fight the Moonlight' fame; I'm sure she still remembers it as warmly as I do). And I'd done an interview with the *Wales on Sunday* newspaper. You could make the case that Ayr is in Scotland rather than Wales, but all it would have taken was for everyone in Wales to call one person in Scotland and tell them. Was that so much to ask?

When we changed trains at Glasgow Central, there was a bit of a setback. As we stood together on a nearly deserted Platform 4, a can of Tennent's lager came flashing through the air and crashed into the wall behind us. If you don't know Tennent's, it's a local brew in Glasgow and very much the sort of lager you would throw across a concourse at someone instead of drinking it. It wouldn't amaze me if, along with the ingredients on the back of the can, there were instructions on how to launch it for maximum distance. If anything, it's almost too much of a cliché to have a can of Tennent's hurled at your head in Glasgow. But this, like all the horrors of this book, was real. The can had been thrown by a dishevelled guy – and that's rich, coming from me – about twenty yards away. The fact he missed is a reminder not to play sport when drunk.

'My God, I'm so sorry, are you OK?' said Chloe, although 'bodyguard' wasn't technically part of her job title. We put some distance between ourselves and the guy – it didn't seem like he'd be into coming to the book launch with us – and got on the Ayr train. One more hour. I imagined the reception at the other end would be a *little* bit warmer. I was both right and wrong.

'Most things don't happen.' Someone said that to me when I was starting out. I can't remember who, now, because I've been doing this long enough and had so many half-recalled post-gig analyses over a drink that my brain is like a charity shop of conversational nuggets.

Not long ago I was asked, in an interview, 'What is the best advice someone's ever given you?' I came out with something about never allowing anyone to make you feel inadequate, but couldn't remember who had given it to me. After it had gone to print, I realised: I'd read the previous column in the interview series to get an idea of what they wanted, and when it came to my turn I had inadvertently recycled the answer given by the previous interviewee. I sometimes wonder if any regular readers noticed.

'Most things don't happen' is from a pool of 'living in the moment' tips that I've picked up over the years and often try to use to take the edge off things – not always successfully since, in a mind as highly strung as mine, 'the edge' is like the blade of one of those kitchen knives my French exchange partner's mum used to swing around. Another, more commonly heard piece of advice is, 'The glass is already broken.' Both of these sound, at worst, quite bleak summaries of our existence and, at best, a half-arsed excuse when you smash a wine glass at a party.

However, if you flip it on its head this aphorism has a troublingly existential ring to it. Most people are people you will never meet. Most of the knowledge assembled by the human race in its complicated history will never be known to you. And most of your projects – your ambitions, the possible directions your life might take – most of these, speaking purely logically, will not happen. There is that whole branch of thought dealing with parallel universes and the idea that, on some plane, every action you declined is being played out by a near-identical version of yourself. I'm a long way away from being able to understand any scientific discussion of matters like this and the philosophical aspect tends to make me feel a bit queasy, as though I'm looking down into the Grand Canyon. But it's true. For every plot point that your life takes, there are hundreds that the scriptwriters reject.

As I said before, we like to believe that our lives are the result of carefully laid plans; that what we get in life is what we work towards and deserve. 'Most things don't happen' is a reminder that it's just not true, because far more comes down to luck, chaos and making things up as we go along. That might feel like a frustrating truth, but it's also an opportunity – to free ourselves of the millstone of our expectations. To go into life with – as near as possible – *no* expectations.

If I'd gone to Ayr that day with no expectations, I would remember it in a much more positive light. It wouldn't need to be logged as another of the great mortifications of my life. And yet . . .

By the time we were pulling into Ayr – at the end of what was now a seven-hour journey to the book event from London – the incident with the can had already passed from an unnerving moment into the realm of 'promising future anecdote'. Chloe and I were making brave little jokes about how we had to hope the guy didn't have a mate who was waiting for us here, perhaps with a more accurate throwing arm.

But no, when we arrived, things were very quiet both on the platform and in the station more generally and on the streets of the pretty coastal town as we walked towards the bookshop. I could only assume everyone had gone early to get the best seats in the house. The town had shut down, as happens for massive World Cup games. Those people who hadn't been able to get tickets would be watching on big screens in nearby bars. Ayr was holding its breath for Mark Watson, the twenty-four-year-old author of a book which had briefly been mentioned on *BBC Breakfast*.

The launch was going to take place not in the store that had organised the event, but in a pub down the road. This seemed like a good idea to me. Bookshops are magical places in all sorts of ways, but they're not necessarily the most atmospheric event venues. It's difficult for a master of ceremonies to shout 'LET'S TAKE THE ROOF OFF!' when they're aware that book-trade profit margins make repairs prohibitively expensive, or to urge the crowd to 'MAKE SOME NOIIIIISE!' when the entire establishment relies on peace and quiet. A pub sounded like a much better bet; people could hang on every word of my reading and also burst into football-style cheering if an adjective really hit the spot. I'd probably be carried shoulder-high around the place if the Q&A segment went well. The only snag was, the place did, at first glance, look – a little bit on the empty side.

The organiser, an amicable older man whose name is now lost to time (in my mind, at least; I assume he himself still remembers it), initially doubled down on the 'fifty to a hundred' prediction, saying, 'We've given out a lot of those flyers and people seemed interested,' which – again, with the benefit of hindsight – was a bit like saying, 'I've invited quite a number of people to the Facebook event' or, 'I said several prayers about it last night.'

As we got closer to the eight o'clock start time, there were still no more than a couple of dozen people in the place. I glanced at the copies of my book arrayed hopefully across a trestle table, theoretically ready for me to sign when people, overwhelmed by the beauty of my prose, queued up to become one of the first readers. This sight – an over-optimistic number of books laid out for sale – would crop up again and again in my publishing career.

'Well,' I said gamely, eyeing the handful of book lovers arranged in ones and twos around their tables, 'I mean, still amazing to have this many people. So far from home and everything. I'm sure it's still going to be fun, if you wanted to crack on . . .'

'Ah,' said the organiser, who was looking a bit older even in the time we had been in the pub. He seemed to have progressed from 'comfortable middle-age' to 'wanting to make the most of the time left'. 'Ah, no, the thing is,' he clarified, 'most of these guys are just . . . having a drink. Your audience is *there*.' He pointed to a space immediately in front of the microphone. On a stool next to the mic was another copy of *Bullet Points*, ready to be scooped up by the man of letters himself.

Around the book and stool sat my audience. There were four people.

Three of them had come together, a forty-something man in an anorak and his aged parents. The other was sitting separately. It was, I registered with surprise, a girl who'd been at my school, a few years below. I looked at the quartet of audience members and then at the increasingly apologetic bookseller. Chloe was swallowing hard, over and over again, as if a piece of spinach had lodged in her throat – not high enough to choke her, but enough to make her uncomfortable, perhaps to wish that she'd gone for the smashed avocado instead. (I should add that this is another anachronistic joke; in 2005 avocado was still very much a minority interest. It would be almost a decade before, globally, we began to subject avocados to the sort of pain we do now.)

'They – they *did* say fifty to a hundred,' said Chloe, faintly, this fabled figure sounding less adjacent to reality every time it was mentioned. Her eyes roved over the ticket-holders – if we can give that title to people attending a free event – and I saw her count and re-count them a couple of times, as if it might be a matter of maths alone; as if, with a bit of creative accounting, there might really be a hundred people instead of four.

'Aye,' said the bookseller, with the air of someone who'd been in conversations about disappointing numbers before. 'We did give out a lot of bits of paper,' he reflected, in retrospect one of the most melancholy statements I've heard from an event organiser – and I've heard plenty of contenders. 'I mean, we could . . . we could give it a few more minutes,' he suggested and all three of us looked out of the window, into the sleepy streets tapering towards the dark, silent Firth of Clyde. The temperature outside was no more than three or four degrees; you could see the breath coming out of the handful of residents who wandered by outside, on their way to a fireside and bed. It didn't immediately look as if dozens of bibliophiles were going to pour out of the shadows.

A low audience count was one thing; it was worse to be outnumbered by people occupying the same room but without the intention of listening to you. And not for the last time: I once performed in a leisure centre where I could see more people bouncing on trampolines than watching the gig. But in Ayr, this was new territory.

I was duly introduced by the bookseller, who thanked everyone for coming out – the word 'everyone' only just grammatically correct here – and I shuffled up to the microphone. The PA system was what I would later come to recognise as a pretty basic set-up but, in fairness, it would probably be more than enough to meet my current needs.

I had, at this point, never MCed a gig. But I'd seen enough to know that it was important to take a sort of census of the crowd. 'So, give me a cheer if you've read the book!' I ventured, bravely. Of course, no one had. 'Or . . . heard about the book on *Breakfast News*, maybe!' Nothing. 'Or in the *Guardian*!' Still nothing. One of the aged parents coughed a little. 'Or – ever heard of me in any way . . .?' Here, the girl from my school put her hand up, which was reassuring, up to a point, but it was hard not to focus on the three other audience members, 75 per cent of the turnout, whose motives for being there were still unaccounted for. I asked them what had brought them to my book-reading, even though – deep down – I already knew the answer.

'We just popped in for a drink and we heard something was going on,' said the elderly lady.

'That's great,' I said, grasping on to this slender encouragement, 'and are you . . . big readers?'

'No, not really,' the lady replied and silence fell again.

Chloe was mortified, the publishers were apologetic and the bookseller bought me a pint (though, looking back, it might well have been Chloe who paid for it). To be fair, the evening was charming. We sat around a table and I awkwardly read the first two pages of the novel. It takes a lot longer than you'd think to read a page of prose out loud, and it feels ten times longer when you're aware that half of the people listening are only doing so because it would be really difficult to walk away in this situation. I then 'took questions', which ranged from 'So, what brings you all the way up here, anyway?' to 'Are you still in touch with any of the teachers from our school?'

Generously, the family-of-three bought a copy of the novel; sometimes I wonder what happened to it, whether it's still in their house somewhere in Scotland or even made it home with them that night. My former schoolmate took another one, and that was the close of business for the night: £15.98 banked by the bookshop, minus the huge runoff of royalties that would soon flow into my account. We thanked the owner and got our bags and went back to the B&B, picking our way through a pub that had got a little busier towards closing time and was now reasonably full of people who had physically attended my first-ever book launch without ever being aware of it.

That night I lay on the bed, picked up the landline to call my parents in Bristol and assured them that, yes, I was, these days, pretty huge on the Scottish literary scene.

Most authors have had an experience like this, especially when starting out. Almost all writers know the feeling of sitting at a table at a book festival waiting to sign copies for people who never come, while at the next table someone else is fighting off readers who say things like, 'You have changed my life,' before staggering off with seventy-two copies in a hessian sack to give to everyone they've ever met. Indeed, I once did an evening of readings that was chaired by a much more famous person and, when it came to the book signing, I saw that the organisers had laid out our books on the same table and seated us side by side. It couldn't have been much more like a competition for the punters' money if they'd rolled pound coins across the table and made us play Hungry Hippos. Of course, far more people bought the famous guy's books than mine. A few of them picked up one of mine too – out of support-iveness or sympathy – but that was almost worse.

One kind lady said, 'I suppose I'd better get your book too, hadn't I?' That's my target audience, I thought, as she shuffled away. People who buy my stuff because they're literally too embarrassed not to.

★

'Build it and they will come.' Someone will very likely have said this to you if you've ever announced a plan to do anything creative but difficult – from making a flick-book to rebuilding the fire-damaged wing of Notre-Dame in Paris. (If it *is* the latter, by the way, get in touch with them first because it looks as if they've already started to sort that out for themselves.)

In the eighties sports classic *Field of Dreams*, Kevin Costner's character hears a voice saying these words and is inspired to turn his cornfield into a baseball stadium. Sure enough, when he carries out this ambitious refurb, famous dead baseball players start to show up, allowing Costner's character (who is called Ray, because it's the eighties) to make a psychological journey towards understanding his relationship with his late father. It's a surprisingly beloved movie, given that the synopsis sounds like a cross between baseball, *DIY SOS* and a zombie horror.

'Build it and they will come' has become a golden rule. Follow your vision, no matter how much scepticism you encounter and how many people called Malcolm show up from the council with planning permission enquiries. Open your 'field of dreams' and the right people will flock to it. Just you watch.

I clung to this as my inspiration over at least the first ten years of my time as a writer and comedian. Regardless of what area we're working in, many of us are motivated by a version of the idea. If we put enough of a shift in, we will eventually be given our due. We'll be recognised for all that effort. We'll get what's owed to us, because otherwise it wouldn't be fair, would it?

And no matter how many times we're told that the world *isn't* fair, that the universe is indifferent, that life is a meaningless trudge towards oblivion – to quote just a few of the fridge magnets I've got in front of me – we struggle to square it with our sense that we're entitled to our just rewards. We feel aggrieved when 'most things don't happen'. Whatever it is that disappoints us in life – overlooked for promotion, a relationship doesn't work out, friend eaten by lion after dare goes disastrously wrong during drunken zoo trip – the disappointment normally stems from a too-rosy vision of what the future would look like; from our vision of the relationship as a series of picnics and sex holidays, or the friend heeding your plea to 'give the lions a miss this time'. We placed ourselves mentally in one of the parallel universes where we got the thing we wanted, all neatly packaged up with a nice bow. And then we've been dragged back into this colder world – the one we actually live in – and it feels like being sent back to school at the end of the summer holidays.

That 'glass is already broken' mentality might sound gloomy, but it is a useful prompt to strap on padding in response to the fact that sometimes you are going to hit the ground hard, because that's just what the world does. Sometimes a foot *is* stuck out maliciously to send us sprawling. But a lot of the time, it's simply the problem we keep coming back to: it's tough out there. And by 'out there' I mean 'everywhere'.

The world might be a big place, but it's not big enough to give out goodies to everyone purely because they wanted those goodies with all their hearts. You only have to look at reality TV – *Britain's Got Talent*, *The Apprentice*, any programme on which people are clawing each other's eyes out to get further in life – to be reminded, painfully, of this. The most common thing you'll hear contestants on such shows come out with, even the hopeless ones, is, 'I just want this so much.'

'This is all I've *ever* wanted,' they might even say, shortly before making a mess of the key change in 'You Raise Me Up' and having a car collect them directly from the stage to take them home. It's part of the appeal of these shows and there is, certainly, a funny side when someone does a piece to camera about wanting to be the next Whitney Houston before singing like a baboon and threatening Simon Cowell with death when he gives them the bad news. But now I've reached the middle age, I find it quite melancholy. These people have been sold the idea that just wanting something more desperately than other people is enough to get them there one day. It's not their fault they bought it: the idea's pushed on us all, constantly. And it just isn't true. The best you can say is, 'If you really, really want something and try extremely hard, you improve your chances of getting it but it's still perfectly possible you won't.' And nobody has a print of that on their living-room wall.

A few years ago, I re-watched *Field of Dreams* and discovered that the quotation is slightly wrong, like so many supposedly iconic movie moments we collectively half remember.

Chief Brody in *Jaws* says, '*You're* going to need a bigger boat' not, '*We're* going to need a bigger boat.' It's an important distinction; Brody's not taking responsibility for the coming carnage, but prophesying it. (He also never says, as people believe, 'Bloody hell, I wish I hadn't gone into the shark-catching business, I'm finding it all quite stressful.') And so it is with *Field of Dreams*. What the hero actually hears is, 'Build it and *he* will come' – 'he' being the father with whom he was never properly reconciled. That's the real goal of the project: to summon just one person.

So if there's a lesson to be taken from the film, it's more abstract than everyone thinks. It's not, 'Set out for success and, hey, here it comes!' It's more like: know why you are doing the things you're doing, see them through as fully as you can, and enjoy what you've got at the end of that process. Even if it isn't everything you ever dreamed of, you can enjoy what it *is*.

It's fair to say that my debut novel *Bullet Points* continued not to set the world alight after that night in Ayr. It struggled to sell many more copies in the rest of the country than it did in that one pub. Actually, there was a misleading moment where it appeared on Amazon's Top

10 new paperbacks chart very shortly after release. The chart is updated hourly, and almost as soon as I refreshed the page it was out of the Top 50; by the time I checked again the next day, it had gone down to No. 412, a chart fall on a scale not seen since the time Sir Paul McCartney made that single with a load of frogs.

My second novel fared considerably worse. The editor who'd signed me, and invested effort and enthusiasm in the first place, left the publishers and handed my new book over to a different editor, who I felt treated it a bit like a stepchild they were annoyed to have to take to the cinema. The book didn't have huge commercial appeal and, by the time it came out, the publishers seemed to me to have already given up on it. The press release might as well have said, 'Well, it is what it is, I suppose.' It sold so few copies that you're more likely to find someone who owns a Jeremy Beadle T-shirt.

By the time I wrote another novel, which I believed (and still do) was much better than the first two, my moment had passed, which is quite a thing to think when you're twenty-six. One day, Francis, the literary agent we met a little while back, called me from Estonia. Francis was – and, I like to think, still is – a kindly, delightful man who had a dog in his office, dined out in restaurants that weren't advertised – and could only be accessed using a code issued in the 1970s – and was always taking himself off to left-field destinations that he couldn't entirely ac-count for. Now that I write all this down, I do question whether he *was* purely a literary agent or spent the greater part of his time working for the secret service.

'What are you doing in Estonia?' I asked.

'Nothing, really,' said Francis. 'I just realised I hadn't been to Tallinn and I thought I should really address that.'

'What did you want to call me about?'

'Oh,' said Francis, 'well, I've just been speaking to Random House about whether they would like to publish future novels.'

'And . . .?'

'And I don't think they would.'

That was that. I never heard directly from the editor again. Three years later, still without a publisher, I ran into them in the street. They greeted me more enthusiastically than you might expect, under the circumstances. 'I've just published a wonderful novel,' they said. 'I'll send you a copy in case you want to recommend it to people.' They were gone then, into the throng of strangers, into the buzz of London, a city that never stops reminding you it doesn't need you. And I remembered how I had felt, only a couple of years ago, on the train to Glasgow, drunk on my first taste of stardom, unaware that someone was waiting for me on the platform with a beer can which might as well have been printed with the words: 'GET OVER YOURSELF'.

Of course, it's a stretch to call this a mortification, or a failure, because even to have been in print so young was a very enviable situation. I wasn't then, and I'm not now, ungrateful for the immense privilege of being published even once, let alone twice. But I did feel that I'd publicly fallen short of what was expected of me, and that quite a lot of people had seen me go over and were laughing behind their hands. I'd had all the hype, the proud parents, the impressed acts backstage going, 'Wow, so I hear you had a book published!' And also the glee of knowing that there would be jealous former uni-mates; the sort of people who were in those anthologies I couldn't get into, who had thought this was their rightful destiny.

Rather than concentrate on what I had been given – two books in print, two more than I would have thought possible at one time – I measured these gifts on a scale like those strongman games at the funfair, where you had to hit something with a mallet, see how high it went and judge yourself accordingly, because we hadn't got the term 'toxic masculinity' yet. On this self-punishing scale, the two published books were only slightly above the ground and well below the targets I felt I ought to have hit – 'massive bestseller' perhaps about halfway up, and 'audience with the Pope, plus Christmas No. 1' at the top.

If you're anything like me, you do this all the time: undermine your achievements by raising the bar the second you've managed to clear it, then clearing *that* only to put the bar up a little bit more. That's fine for competitors in sport, where we get the expression from – if you're a pole-vaulter and you're *not* 'raising the bar' quite often, you've probably not understood very well how the sport works. But we aren't meant to live as if every day is the Olympics. Pressing on and on towards ever greater things is a good mentality to have up to a point, but it can also create a sort of spiritual adrenaline-thirst that can never be quenched. It's back to that problem of thinking, What's next, then? when you've barely finished, let alone enjoyed your current endeavour.

If you live – as I have far too often – with this mindset ('Forget the times I managed A, B, C, D and everything up to about J; what would be *really* good is if I could just do K and L') then you'll be pushing the bar upwards forever, and one day you will slam your knees against it and come crashing down. And life doesn't normally provide those nice crash mats they have in athletic competitions. Life's floor can be pretty unforgiving.

A couple of years after the conversation in which Francis gently released me from my bestselling-author aspirations, I was doing a supermarket shop. As I fiddled with my iPhone, which at the time was new technology and felt like a magic wand, I heard a surprised cry. I looked up to see a young man with a book in front of me. My first thought was that it was an unusual move to bring a book to the supermarket; I could only conclude either that it was some sort of affectation or that he was absolutely hooked on whatever he was reading. It was *my* novel, the one I premiered so spectacularly in Ayr. We stared at each other.

'It's you!' he said.

I didn't dispute it.

It must have looked to him for a second as though I had somehow done this on purpose; as though I was in the habit of finding out every time somebody purchased a copy, discovering their location and showing up in person pleading for compliments. (As you now know, this wouldn't actually have taken very long.)

'I'm sorry to startle you,' I said, 'it's just – well, I've never seen anyone actually reading it! Like, in real life.'

'I would have thought it would happen all the time,' he said, with a respect that I found touching. I didn't want him to sense how wrong he was, so I aimed for a sort of mysterious laugh. Not being much of an actor without the safety net of tights and talcum powder, I produced something which sounded a bit like the mangled chuckle of a hotelier ridiculing Poirot's concerns about the safety of his establishment, ten minutes before someone is found with an ice pick in his spine. 'Well, I'm really loving it,' said the reader, instantly becoming my favourite person I had ever met in a supermarket (and I worked on a checkout for two years, although not every customer was a contender, shall we say). 'It's really made me think and moved me,' he said.

This was the sort of reader encounter you have in your daydreams, but you never think you'll see it actually happen, much as a comedian of my level rarely has someone come and say, 'I love your work, I consider you to be a lot better than all these people who massively outsell you – that is just the idiocy of the general public for you – and I definitely do not have you confused with Chris O'Dowd.'

But now it was happening. All my instincts were to dismiss the compliment – or, if not dismiss it, play it down and talk the way I've been talking about the novel for most of this chapter. 'Oh, really? *Nobody* read that. Actually, the day of the first book event I only sold two more copies than I had cans of lager chucked at my head.'

I don't think this urge is purely a neurotic comedian thing, either. Most of us are in the habit of reflexively batting away compliments. 'Oh, dinner was nothing special, don't be silly.' 'What, this dress? I found it in a skip.' It comes from a perhaps quite likeable instinct not to come over as being too big-headed, to wear praise lightly, but if you do this long enough, you can easily start to believe that your qualities really are as disposable as your chat suggests.

'Argue for your failings, and they're yours,' I read once. It's true. If you keep saying out loud that you're not really up to much, you quickly internalise that as a genuine belief. It's like that clichéd-sounding – but true – principle that if you make yourself smile and laugh, you experience a chemical boost as if the happiness you are faking were real. In the years since my books came out, I'd said the equivalent of, 'Well, I was never going to make it as an author anyway,' so many times that it was now rubber-stamped across my entire being.

This time, I didn't say any of these things; I didn't even make a self-effacing remark of the kind that rolls so easily off the tongue. I just thanked him, sincerely, said that I hoped he enjoyed the rest of it, shook his hand, and we went our separate ways. But I'd learned something in that two-minute conversation/accidental stalking of my readership which ought to have been obvious, yet it had failed to form in my brain in the previous two or three years of self-pity.

I hadn't been writing books for millions of people to buy and then for those readers to send me fan mail, put up statues of me in their gardens and offer me free use of their holiday home on a breathtaking Greek island. Don't get me wrong: all this would be nice and, audience-wise, it might be quite useful to break into that demographic of 'people with private island access'. These things, though, were peripheral to the actual business of making or doing something just because you wanted to make or do it. The young me wasn't jealous of cult vegetable author Jayne Fisher because she'd sold a million copies or Aled Jones because he'd earned a million pounds; the young me didn't have a clue about that stuff. He, I, just wanted to be one of those people who had done something which found an audience. Done something which someone else cared about. That encounter in the supermarket reminded me that I had become 'one of those people'. I had made a thing and another person had enjoyed it. I just had to allow myself to feel that.

After all, the whole thing about books is that they knock about for an awfully long time. Some of your favourite books were probably written by people who missed out on seeing you read them by a century or more. When I had my Chaucer obsession at university, part of the appeal was that I couldn't get over the idea somebody could have been living six hundred years before me, in a world utterly different from mine, a man who never went to a football match, ate chorizo or saw *Gogglebox* – as far as we know – and yet, through his words on a page he was able to crack a rude joke which made me laugh down the centuries.

And, of course, Chaucer was one of the lucky ones. Plenty of authors, plenty of other creators, do a Vincent van Gogh and never get anywhere till well after their lives are over, which is arguably a bit late to start enjoying things. One of my favourite novels, *The Third Policeman*, by Flann O'Brien, was rejected by publishers because it was too weird (and it *is* weird, I agree). He died, drunk and disappointed, having hidden the manuscript and claimed he'd lost it – which is a harder trick to get away with these days. It wasn't until he was long in the ground – thirty-one years afterwards – that I received a copy of his masterpiece from my uncle Geoff and fell in love with it. Can you imagine what Flann O'Brien would say if he could come back for a day and find that his work had found its readers after all, not just with me but with a cult following of thousands – even more since a character was seen reading it in the TV series *Lost*? I think I can: he'd say, 'For fuck's sake, that makes it even worse; if you idiots had just listened to me I wouldn't have gone to my grave with this feeling of injustice. God, I wish I'd never accepted that invitation to come back for a day.'

But you see my point. A book is a conversation between you – the writer – and a single person. In O'Brien's case: me. In my case: a surprised man in Londis. If someone had asked me, as an aspiring writer: would you be happy if just one person read your work and cared about it? I would have said, 'Of course.'

Because, when it came down to it, whatever activity you took on, you did it for yourself; you thought of something that you'd want to exist, and you set about making it exist. You had a tune in your head and you played it on the guitar or, if you're my next-door neighbour, some sort of weird harpsichord thing which you're hopefully going to sell soon. You read a popular post which you thought took a misleadingly shallow glance at a complex issue (I know, hard to imagine, but it *can* happen), and patiently wrote a long thread setting the record straight. You looked at a papier-mâché swan in the window of a craft shop and thought, I could do better than that, that's all out of proportion; a black swan's wingspan is about 1.8 metres, for God's sake. You wanted to sit back and look at the thing you had produced and say: the world now has this piece of work in it and, even if I'm not entirely satisfied with it – even if the beak was a lot more challenging than I anticipated – I did it. You did not think, This swan is going to change the game globally. People will stop me in the street. Will.i.am will tweet about it. All these things are peripheral.

Bands quite often talk about how they 'really just make music for ourselves, y'know, and if anyone likes it that's cool'. It's quite easy to sneer at this sort of thing. Partly because it sounds disingenuous. If you don't care whether anyone listens to your music, the obvious question is: why go to the considerable trouble of recording, publishing and advertising it? It seems as much of a contradiction as those roundups of 'photos this celebrity didn't want you to see!' which the celeb's PR team has clearly accidentally put together and accidentally sent out to all major news outlets. But the band's philosophy *does* have a certain truth in it, even if you wish they would speak up a bit and stop glowering at the camera like they're being photographed before being taken into custody. The only person you can actually make stuff for is, on some level, yourself. As soon as it's out in the world it can be misunderstood, under-appreciated, lost altogether. Those things won't be your fault, but they will feel like they are. So, treasure the thing you've done, whatever it is, for its own sake – not for the attention it might bring you. Focus on the thing it is, not the other things it might lead to.

This isn't just true of creative projects. Whatever you are doing in life, you need to be doing it because it answers some hunger you have, in and of itself. You cannot trust this bad world to validate you – in a way you shouldn't even want that. You should be doing things because you take your *own* validation from them. That goes beyond fancy stuff like writing books or posting your art on Instagram or making a massive papier-mâché swan. It's something you owe yourself, no matter your lifestyle. In your relationships with other people, in your day-to-day work, in everything. You can't control what happens to your output, whether people care about it or not. All you can control is whether *you* care about it. And that's all you should be thinking about.

To come back to *Field of Dreams*, then: build it – whatever form 'it' takes – and they *might* come. But if they don't, be prepared to run around the baseball diamond on your own and bloody well enjoy it. You built that thing and it took ages and you got mud all over you, and Malcolm from the council kept making weird remarks about what he'd had for breakfast during your planning permission emails, because he's one of these people who mistake official correspondence for Facebook Messenger. Getting anything done in this life, pursuing anything with any seriousness, is hard and draining and takes commitment. You can't be waiting around for other people to give you permission to feel good about the decisions you've made. You have to give yourself that permission.

If you don't – if you go through life waiting for people to notice and say, 'Well done,' like me refreshing my sales numbers for that first book and counting the unsold copies on the way back from Ayr — you'll end up making more decisions in the hope of pleasing those people, rather than yourself. The consequences of this are pretty serious, as I've learned to my cost. So let's go there, shall we?

4

I SHOULDN'T BE HERE

I'm on the set of a panel show, one of many such sets on which I have found myself sitting at a fake desk with a buzzer in front of me. It doesn't matter which show, but you'll have seen it, and you can easily conjure the general aesthetic in your head. Big, bold colours; almost children's TV-esque. Wisecrackers, mostly men, mostly in suits, sitting in an unnatural row, like delegates at the United Nations. A household name presiding over proceedings. A neurotic producer, in a not-quite-as-good suit, bustling on set every now and again to suggest some one-liners he'd really like to see spontaneously bursting out of the comedians. Hair and make-up people flitting in and out of the shadows with brushes, lint rollers and spray canisters, making little adjustments to the very important men. A powerful gantry of lights beaming in the eyes of all the participants, reminiscent of Hollywood interrogation scenes.

An audience of about two hundred – though the cameras have been set up to make it look like far more

– are howling and clapping with delight at pretty much everything anyone says, especially the words of the more famous guests. Partly because they *are* delighted, and partly because they have been drilled to do this both by a warm-up man who spent the first fifteen minutes of the evening whipping the enthusiasm into a froth and by the neurotic producer who wanders on at the start and says, pitifully, things like, 'Let's have big smiling faces, let's have loud laughs!' Each one of the crowd is fitted with a sensor that uses Bluetooth to send a minute-by-minute laughter graph to the production team and, if their laugh levels drop below a certain point, they are escorted out of the building at gunpoint. (I made the last bit up, of course, but it isn't as much of an exaggeration as it should be.)

On this particular set, on this particular evening, the work is almost done. But there's one more thing left to film: a charity appeal, because this episode is going out in the middle of TV fundraising season. The host, one of the most famous comedians in the country, just has to read a brief piece to camera explaining where viewers' money will go.

I'm looking forward to the show being over. It has been, not for the first time, a fairly difficult evening for me on set. I have made maybe two or three meaningful contributions in three hours (these recordings are devilishly long, typically five times the length of the eventual broadcast episode). One of the show's regulars glared across the room as I began an anecdote, I lost my nerve and messed it up; one of my jokes was reworked by another comic later in the recording and I know it'll be his version that is used in the edit because he's also one of the show's core team.

All this is fairly standard. It's part of what my career is these days. In my heart, I know that it is not exactly what I set out to do. The cold precision of a TV set is much less my habitat than an intimate arts theatre, or the tiny but beloved study in the flat I now live in. The gladiatorial medium and the super-topical emphasis are both some distance away from my specialist area, which is telling long stories about my own life. In fact, a lot of the professional things I'm proudest of are almost the antithesis of these cunningly produced entertainment formats.

I've made my name at the Edinburgh Fringe with a series of madly long shows. The original one was twenty-four hours, culminating in my proposing to my girlfriend (successfully, although she had very little room to decline). We went up to twenty-seven and even thirty-six hours in subsequent years. Other avant-garde projects have involved marching people around the city, planting trees, commandeering a church to stage a fake wedding ceremony, and organising a comedians' Olympics to determine who's best at throwing fruit into a bucket or putting on multiple garments. All these shows are about collaboration and chaos. They're the opposite of competitive (except the bit with the fruit-throwing). They're attempts to establish community; I'm just the conduit for unexpected synergies between comedians and comedy-watchers. Even my more conventional stand-up shows lean heavily on interaction with the audience, go off-piste at every opportunity, change from night to night. The things I do best are the opposite of what these TV blockbusters demand.

But the TV shows are working. I'm selling tickets to tour shows; people know my name; taxi drivers never fail to give me their verdict. And my manager – who took me on after that early *Daily Telegraph* award – is delighted with the progress I'm making. The relationship between manager and performer is a symbiotic one. You're like two people doing one of those tandem skydives. If one of you does something stupid, both of you are going to crash. If you cling on to each other, if you react as one, you might just land safely. Except, of course, entertainment is about trying *not* to land. It is best thought of as a skydive in which you and your professional partner try to remain airborne, eternally, for the benefit of people standing and clapping on the ground below. You tell each other you're still in the air, you're still doing well, people are loving it and you make each other believe it. My manager was one of the best in the business at doing this, and we were flying pretty nicely.

On this occasion, though – as usual with these engagements – I'm keen to return to the dressing room and put my real clothes on, getting out of what I am currently wearing: clothes that the show's stylist has chosen to reflect 'my look', by examining photographs of my usual wardrobe and then buying things that are almost identical but more expensive.

There's just this little bit of admin – the charity appeal – to complete. The host has to read the words, 'Every five seconds, a child dies in poverty' while we all look down the barrel of the camera and remind people in lower-income brackets that it's time to dig deep to redress injustice. We're all used to recording these after-hours snippets; we're all professionals. Actually, there's one popular panel show which is such a gruelling experience for the participants that when the recordings finish, all the comedians have to sit and laugh out loud into thin air for five minutes while the cameras record. Those clips can be thrown into the edit to make it look as if we were all cackling at each other's jokes. That's right: we are *our own* canned laughter. When studio audience members witness it for the first time, you can see a little bit of their hearts dying.

The millionaire to my right, the host, says, 'Every five seconds, a poverty . . .' Oops! He's messed it up. The audience laugh, scandalised. Nothing makes an audience happier than getting a glimpse of something going wrong; a peek behind the flatscreen of their TV, the moment they would never have been privy to if they were among the masses watching at home. This happens every time and it's understandable. These TV shows are so slick and so polished when you see them on the screen; there's a human joy in seeing the cracks, turning to your family and saying, 'Well, actually, I was at the recording, and . . .'

That love of chaos is hardwired into us all; it's perhaps why we treasure comedy in the first place, our relish of order being subverted, authority being undermined. I was once part of the bill on a show where part of the set fell down behind one of the other comedians, and it was one of the biggest ovations I've ever seen in a theatre. It was a useful, if deflating, lesson: don't get too cocky, you can always be upstaged by a piece of scenery.

'Every five seconds . . .' begins the celebrity again, but no, he's got the giggles. Again, he fluffs the line about all the deaths of the unfortunate children. Again, the audience absolutely love it. And in a sense, we aren't hurting anyone. No impoverished child is actually getting deprived of food *because* of this unsavoury scene. The charity appeal will get recorded, it will be broadcast, people will donate or they won't. It's just, for me, something about it is a bit 'last days of the Roman Empire': well-paid men making a slapstick routine out of world inequality, liberal audience members losing their shit in amusement. It's not just that the overall spectacle makes me feel queasy; it's that I'm actively participating in it. I'm not standing up for what I believe in. I'm just trimming off those areas of my personality to fit into this box. 'The box' being not just this studio, but the TV that pretty much everyone in the country has in their living room.

It flashes across my mind: *I shouldn't be here.* The thought has been chewing away at the edges of my brain the whole night, but there's nothing I can do about it at this late stage and I doubt I'll do anything about it next time, even though I do have the option of saying, 'No, thank you, I don't want to be booked for that show again.'

After all, it's not as if I haven't had this feeling before. I've been ignoring it for years now; it, and every other feeling that was meant to tell me something important.

I shouldn't be here is a feeling you will have experienced before, perhaps multiple times if your decision-making is anything like mine. Maybe it was the time you were standing on a diving board, twenty metres up in the air, having only come up here in the first place because your mates were all doing it, and you realised, as you gazed down at the distant pool. It might have been in the opening five minutes of the cinema release of *Cats*. Or that time your cousin persuaded you to explore that supposedly disused snake pit in the Mojave Desert and to leave your phone at home to 'make the experience more authentic'.

Sometimes these gut-lurches are purely instinctive, our hardware firing up the fight-or-flight mechanisms that prevented us from getting gored by mammoths or sitting through an ill-considered cinematic reworking of a very specifically theatrical experience. Sometimes those spurts of chemical activity can be safely ignored, because we've evolved a long way as a species. We understand that, actually, leaping into a swimming pool will probably *not* put our lives in danger (although I do always imagine cracking my head on the lower board; there's a YouTube clip that is very difficult to dispel from the mind). The near-panic experienced by a new comedian when they look out at three hundred complete strangers is a necessary, useful adrenaline-spike that can be channelled into the right kind of energy – not an *actual* warning that there are three hundred potential killers here, unless the gig is in Maidstone.

However, sometimes *I shouldn't be here* speaks to you on a deeper level. It demands to be heard. And if you don't listen, you're heading for much bigger trouble than having gone to see a film that ill-advisedly tries to stretch a supernatural cat plot for two hours.

The moving charity appeal is recorded at last for the panel show and the people watching at home on Thursday night will see only the sincere, straight-faced appeal from the megastar: '*Your* money can make a difference to people with really tough lives.' The last studio audience members have been evacuated from the building, although a few of the properly devoted ones will linger around the stage door hoping to get selfies, unaware that the most famous people have already been guided out through a different, selfie-proof exit. I'm in the green room having a glass of wine or, more realistically, several, to put some space between myself and the events of the evening. But this hasn't been an isolated incident. My montage of TV *I shouldn't be here* moments is a long one, soundtracked by the sort of power ballad that they use on the closing TV segment when England go out of a major tournament on penalties. We only have time for a couple of lowlights.

I'm in another panel show studio, on a row of six men (we still haven't invented women). I'm the only one who isn't a regular. When we were all brought out, the audience screeched their approval at the first five, then clapped politely like a county cricket crowd when it was my turn. As the microphones were being tested, there was some banter between two of the other guests, which went down an absolute storm; the pair of them were in the audience's good books before we had even started recording. I'd tried to join in with the riff and, in front of the whole audience, killed it stone dead, like the bore on Twitter who repeats your own gag back at you. When, finally, we did get on camera, my first joke, naturally, died. I could feel in the silence the thing a comedian perhaps dreads more than booing, more than indifference: pity. Everyone wants me to say something funny; they want it almost as much as I do. But the more that thought nags at me, the more I try to be funny, the less funny I become. It's not as if there's any shortage of funny stuff flying about, anyway. The other comics have very much got it covered. They're all talented gagsmiths and the most popular of them actually has a team who have crafted for him several A4 pages of the searing put-downs he's so famous for creating. There's very, very little I can bring to the party and, if it *were* a party, I'd be the guy near the stereo whose friends are climbing all over each other, but I've got no way of getting home because I'd been assured one of them could 'definitely give me a lift back'.

But what's this? Something is happening behind us. There's some activity in the studio; the floor manager has stepped in and paused the recording. We all glance behind us. There are large clouds of dry ice drifting on to the set. The machine that pumps out the substance at the start of the show – to make the audience feel a little more like they're stepping into a magical otherworld – is malfunctioning and has suddenly started belching out enough smoke to give the impression the whole place is in flames. Here's a chance for me to say something funny, even if there's no way it can actually be broadcast.

'I think the main news of the week is that our building's on fire,' I observe.

The studio audience love it. Of course, they do; once again, it's the in-joke effect; they've witnessed that thing they weren't meant to see. With that first big laugh, I can hear myself exhale, feel my heart rate return from its helpless clatter to the normal, functional speed a heart beats at when you're not spending two hours trying to salvage your reputation in front of two hundred people. It's all going to be all right. It's a shame my one moment of wit can't be included in the actual show because the cameras have stopped rolling and the style people have moved in to pick things out of our hair and rub their mysterious rollers over us, but it's changed my status in the room. I can build on this.

We're given a five-minute break; we all stand up, stretch our legs, exchange brief pleasantries about how things are going. Then we settle back down into our seats, the particularly big-name comic glancing over the gags his little team of writers has supplied about the thoughts he's supposedly had in the past week. The warm-up man returns to the floor, hollers into his microphone that he needs everyone to go crazy. The members of the studio audience, who by now have long forgotten the lives they had before they came into this sweaty room, oblige with some authentic-sounding whooping and stamping. The cameras are rolling again. There is still a very noticeable amount of smoke in the air.

The host reads a little link off the autocue, we're back in. Another comedian immediately says, 'Well, I think the main news story is that our building's on fire!' Of course, the place immediately erupts, because everyone is in on it: the joke is funnier as a re-tread of itself – a 'callback', as it's known in comedy. And they appreciate the extra dimension, too: the audacity of the other comic having *literally stolen it from me* in front of their eyes. Even I appreciate it, in a way. But it is *slightly* like having a doughnut in your hand, and then having someone pluck it from your hand and eat it before your eyes, only for lots of people to say, 'I thought that was brilliant, the way the guy had the idea of eating that doughnut. He's so quick! We should get tickets to go and see him eating doughnuts in a venue near us.'

Jump ahead a year. I'm on another panel show. You've seen this one, as well, although it isn't on TV anymore; it was put out of its misery a mere eleven or so series after it stopped being funny. This time, I have a stomach bug and I don't think it's unlikely I'm going to throw up reasonably soon. Under the clammy lights, in the heat, I feel the room swimming slightly.

I did tell my manager, earlier in the afternoon, that I wasn't 'quite feeling right' – to use one of the many comforting euphemisms for 'I absolutely have the shits'. Truth be told, about two hours before we went on camera, I felt rough enough to try to pull out of the show. But from my manager's point of view pulling out would, of course, be a disaster. You have to be literally dead before you are able to excuse yourself from a TV recording on the day and even then they would probably prop you up, *Weekend at Bernie's*-style, and have an impressionist chip in as you from under the desk. Something like that would scar my future. The production company would be pissed off with me; I would be put on a blacklist; next time they were looking for someone to make up the numbers on their show, they would bypass me in favour of a less nauseous figure.

And so, I get through the evening, a long way below top form, at the mercy of the often very harsh criticism you can get for daring to appear on TV, because doing this compromised, miserable version of my job feels preferable to admitting the impossible: that *I should not be here*.

Again and again during this period, if a potential gig stirred up difficulties – childcare problems, massive travel stress, clashes with a friend's funeral, this sort of thing – it would be put to me that if I didn't grab the moment, if I prioritised anything that wasn't breaking my neck to get to a studio, I would not just be wasting an opportunity but gift-wrapping it for a rival. It was a poisonous mindset to adopt, but I don't blame any of the people who prompted me to do so. Your frame of mind is ultimately your own responsibility, just like the state of your kitchen.

The point is that I was living almost exclusively to meet other people's expectations. Almost every decision I made was to stop somebody from being angry or disappointed with me, or to chase some stick that someone was throwing for me. I was going back, again and again, to environments in which I didn't particularly belong and where I often felt uneasy. I had to earn a living, of course, but it wasn't as if I'd starve if I stopped doing these particular shows and, anyway, it wasn't really about that. It was about the fact that I was blocking out the *I shouldn't be here* alarm; in fact, I'd taken the batteries out altogether. This is sometimes necessary if you have, for example, a smoke alarm anything like mine – it's so overzealous that after a while you think, I'll take my chances on asphyxiation if it means I can fry sausages without fear. But there are some alarms you definitely shouldn't turn off.

★

Life's most important flashing red lights aren't the ones that blind you when you're looking down the barrel of a physically terrifying task, like a skydive. Those are animal impulses and they might well not line up with what's actually happening. The alarms you need to heed aren't jabbing at you like needles. They're more like a recurring headache or a dull pain in your stomach; they come back again and again.

These moments, though, are just widely spaced enough that you believe each time that it's a one-off, that you're just 'not quite yourself'. If you do this for long enough, the definition of 'yourself' begins to change, as you try to make what you're saying become the truth. You start to live like an actor playing the role of you. Something is missing inside. But outward appearances convince people and that image has started to be all you really care about. You can go on like that for years without confronting the harder job of looking at what's beneath.

Living for other people is one of the easiest ways you can lose sight of who you actually set out to be. I don't, of course, mean living in a way that makes others' lives better, taking care of them, being selfless. I'm not sure there's a gap in the market for a self-help book that says, 'FORGET YOUR CHARITABLE IMPULSES, SCREW EVERYTHING AND EVERYONE, TRAMPLE YOUR WAY TO THE TOP OF A HEAP OF BODIES!' It's not necessary when so many of the world's governments and its most vocal corporations are implicitly saying that already. What

I *am* warning against is doing what I did for far too much of my late twenties and thirties: performing a version of myself in an attempt to make people happy.

This is obviously a particular danger when you are in a field like mine, which almost literally consists of going from one room to the next shouting, 'Do you like me? Exactly how much do you like me? What could I do that might make you like me more?' (A friend of mine observed years ago that expecting to earn a living from performing is, in a way, akin to going into a corner shop, doing a somersault and demanding a can of beans.) If you have a job that consists of trying to second-guess what people want and if, as part of that job, you have a management team whose entire modus operandi is to stalk the kingmakers of the industry to find out what they want and email you saying things like, 'The new Channel 4 guy is obsessed with golf, do you have a golf sitcom idea?' . . . well, it's not surprising that you start to become unhealthily focused on making decisions that might lead to popularity, rather than peace of mind, because you've started to conflate the two. But you don't have to be Krusty the Clown to realise that, without even being aware of it, you've fallen into the trap of living a life that's mostly a desperate chase for applause.

The house you live in. The relationship you commit to. The job you do. All these are negotiations between what you actually – deep down – want, and the things that people either want for you or at least make you feel you're meant to aspire to.

Sometimes in life there are clear examples of people trying to convince you that their own desires and plans are actually what you want for yourself. A friend's father inflicted long-term trauma by saying, 'What's that? You're gifted at music and art so you're thinking of doing music and art A-levels and going down some sort of creative path? Well, that's lovely, but the thing is, I'm a doctor, so I think it's probably best if you become a doctor too; I've put you down for chemistry and snapped all your pencils.' (I'm only partly exaggerating.)

More commonly, though, when people ask things of you, they're asking because they genuinely think it's in your interests. Those same cheerleaders who leaned into your freshers' week, shouting, 'Greatest days of your life! Found your twenty best friends of all time yet?' are still at the side of the road as you round the bends into the stages of life that follow. The problem is, in many cases they do *not* know what's best for you. You do. You just might not be listening to yourself.

Now, none of this is meant to imply that the reason I did a damaging number of panel shows – and quite a few things I was even less suited to – was that others dragged me into doing them. I hope it will be clear throughout that the key architect of my own misfortune has been me.

And it's hardly as if I was doing anything that every-one else wasn't doing. Especially everyone else who was a middle-class, nicely educated man with a selection of indie band T-shirts and a repertoire of reasonably safe observations about the difficulties of predictive texting. The fact is, at the very time I was starting to surf the wave of stand-up, it had become the biggest wave around. Comedy had never been as much of a boom industry in this country as it was in the seven or so years after I began, in 2002. There had always been topical news shows, of course, but all of a sudden there was a craze for them and, once the fire had been lit, it was only going to spread, because TV commissioners live in a permanent cycle of seeing what the other channels are doing, desperately trying to copy it and then claiming the resulting show 'is what we've always been about as a channel' – unless it flops, in which case it never happened. (I was once in a meeting with an executive who said, 'What we'd really, really love is something like *Peep Show*,' and, when I asked a couple of basic questions, it became obvious he had never seen *Peep Show*. He just meant, as people in TV always do, 'What I'd really, really like is to do something successful.')

What this imitative feeding frenzy meant was that, almost overnight, a couple of dozen, fairly young, virtually all male stand-ups became household names and, for a while, I was one of them. Although by comparison with the show regulars my 'household' of fame was probably only a bungalow or something, it was still a lot more than I'd ever imagined I would be getting, particularly as I was comparatively new to all this. Being a stand-up in the latter part of the decade which people unfortunately managed to label the 'noughties' felt like being a prospector in the USA in the late 1840s. And the landscape of television was totally different, too. We were not yet all enslaved to Netflix, with its forty-eight hours of new drama every day, with its thirty-part series beginning at the rate of one every five minutes, a new episode starting even as the credits are rolling on the previous one, an email notifying you that your subscription will be cut off if you get any further behind with *Schitt's Creek*.

In 2010, there was still a general attachment to the idea of watching what was on the terrestrial channels and at the time they were broadcast rather than, like the power-mad kings and queens we all are these days, at whatever time of day or night it pleases us. If you were on a show like *Mock the Week*, people would nudge and glance at you on the tube the next day, or they might surreptitiously google you on their iPhone. Sometimes it wasn't so surreptitious, actually; sometimes I would be walking along and a man would see fit to lean out of a window and yell, '*8 OUT OF 10 CATS!*' as if I were suffering from an exceptional short-term memory defect and relied on strangers sum-marising my every move by street telegram. Alternatively, if they were slightly less clued-up or more drunk, they might just shout, 'IT'S YOU, IT'S YOU, OI, MATE, ISN'T IT? MATE!'

The attention of what my grandma would have called 'every Tom, Dick and Harry' had its downsides, of course – sometimes it's quite nice to eat a sandwich or have a wee without it being seen as 'material'. But, as I'm sure goes without saying, it had much more substantial upsides. With the enhanced profile of a 'TV personality', I was suddenly promoted beyond bread-and-butter circuit gigs – the student unions and the back rooms of pubs – to the more lucrative and kudos-laden world of theatre touring. I had a bit of money; I had *fans*. People started to pre-book my Edinburgh shows; I would arrive at venues to see the intoxicating splash of a 'SOLD OUT' sign pasted across my face on the advertising material. I started to get opportunities to perform abroad. I was performing in Melbourne on the third anniversary of my Maidstone nightmare; I did two weeks at the Sydney Opera House (not the main room, it must be said, but history doesn't need to record that).

The wellspring of all this seemed to be TV shows. And so, I kept on doing them, even the ones that punched down mercilessly at the less fortunate, or involved hours of being talked over, or made victims out of other people in the room. These shows were not where I believed my talents really lay, but they were a very successful means to an end. Unfortunately, it wasn't long before I mistook them for an end in themselves.

As my public perch grew more visible, so did the ability of the viewers to knock me off it with comments posted online: sometimes with a gentle mockery, but sometimes by taking a chainsaw to the perch and its entire support-ing structure and watching me plummet skull-first to the ground. The phenomenon of social media was still fairly new and I didn't yet know how to disengage from it, so I came to be more and more painfully conscious of the invisible enemies out to get me. I would sense them scratching at the walls even as the episode was being aired, arms folded sceptically like Statler and Waldorf, the two heckling innovators up in the posh box in the Muppets' theatre. It wasn't just pure paranoia; there were plenty of them out there.

After one high-profile TV appearance somebody on Twitter said, 'I'm a fan, and I thought you were awful.' Another person, who'd been to see me in a big theatre venue – where the audience, by and large, seemed to enjoy themselves – tweeted to say they 'had been looking forward to it and were fully and totally disappointed'. The day after a DVD recording someone who'd been at a gig (for free) sent me a Facebook message saying, 'It isn't really your fault, but you are incredibly mediocre.' When a sitcom pilot of mine didn't do the trick for somebody on a comedy forum, they wrote, 'Fuck you, Mark Watson, for letting me down.' And, shortly after I had mentioned on a national TV show that my then wife was pregnant, a well-wisher took to Twitter to say, 'I bet your wife hopes your baby is stillborn if you're the dad.' I'd always been aware that speedy feedback came with the territory; but social media changed that territory. Now, the feedback was instant, and it was everywhere at once.

If your sense of self is well-grounded – if its foundations are in your friends and family and/or in a feeling that you are satisfied in your work, regardless of others' response – it is easier to deal with this sort of stuff, even the appalling latter example. Plenty of comedians, especially women, deal with worse than this on a weekly basis. But I was nowhere near having that sort of grounding at that point. I had based my sense of self so purely on the approval of others that, when that approval was withdrawn, I didn't know how to replace it.

What was left was a void. Voids, I think it's fair to say, are rarely good news. You won't often hear someone say, 'Congratulations, I heard about the void in your soul' or even, 'There is a gigantic void in my diary and I couldn't be happier.' And, as we'll see, the ways I tried to fill the void would lead to far more complicated problems than feeling I was about to throw up in a TV studio.

The people who had high hopes for me – friends, family, managers – were all acting with good or at least under-standable intentions. The people in your life who want you to succeed, settle down or win Wimbledon – or whatever success might be – are not deliberately heaping pressure on your shoulders. The vast majority of people cheering you on in life are doing it because they are excit-ed by your story, rooting for you the way we root for the characters in reality shows, who are desperately trying to find love or make a layer cake which is sufficiently like the

Hanging Gardens of Babylon to draw a handshake from Paul Hollywood.

This is especially true of parents and more senior family members whose lives may have plateaued somewhat, excitement-wise, and who are now ploughing their spare energies into living *your* ups and downs vicariously. And they deserve it. They carried you on their shoulders up seven hundred steps that time at St Paul's Cathedral because you were having a tantrum; they drove fifty miles to pick you up from that party in Wiltshire because you were fifteen and had misunderstood how Southern Comfort is meant to be consumed. You cannot begrudge these people that. And if, like me, you're lucky enough to have a small group of fans, or anybody who appreciates the work that you do – whatever that work is – you owe them all the gratitude you can possibly muster, for making what you do meaningful. Even if, like that po-faced band in the flour mill, you didn't set off specifically to get their attention.

But you do *not* owe it to anybody – not even those closest to you – to live the life they think you ought to have. You don't need to match up to an idea they have of you, or to tick achievements off a list they made in their heads. It's good to try to make your life as nourishing of other people as possible; it's an excellent use of your time on this strange blue-green orb to maximise the happiness of as many other people living on it as you possibly can. But you are not living your life *for* other people; that isn't possible. Nobody else is waking up as you, pulling your trousers on, putting bread in your toaster (well, someone could theoretically be doing the last two of those, but if they are, you need to ask some questions). You are not living your life for the applause or approval of others. You are not trying to get higher and higher on a leaderboard that somebody else is updating. Your job in life, when it comes down to it, is to win your *own* approval.

These are all things you instinctively know already, but sometimes it's good to be reminded of them. I could have done with somebody saying it to me in my late twenties, that's for sure. We spend so much of life trying to do what we think other people expect of us. And when we're not trying to please others, we're comparing ourselves endlessly with them — trying to live by their measures rather than our own.

This last pitfall is the one we're going to discuss next. As pits go, it is a particularly deep one, and the tumble down it was a neck-breaker.

5

LIVING DEATH

The wind is howling around my face as I get off the train at Skegness station, and it continues to pick up off the water as I walk to the Embassy Theatre, which backs on to a deserted funfair and the sad-looking beach itself. Skegness, or 'Skeggy', is the sort of place reputations go to die. It's a seaside resort perched on the edge of the strange, humped bit of the east coast of England before you really get to the north. The peak of its fame was as the home of the first-ever Butlins holiday camp, which, in the fifties and sixties, was a beloved cheap family destination. The war wasn't long over and, even on their holidays, people were still reasonably happy with being shouted at to get up in the morning. Like almost all seaside towns in the UK, Skegness has fallen on hard times in the past few decades, because the price of international flights fell steeply and the nation collectively worked out that, compared with almost all other countries to its south, Britain isn't a very good place to put a beach.

This story isn't tailored to be told at the expense of Skegness, even though it's an easy target. As with 'Cangate' in
Glasgow, I would have preferred that the setting had been
different. Lord only knows, as I plod through Skegness's
already dark and deserted streets, with just the pitying
squawk of seabirds for company, there are any number of
other 'settings' I'd swap this for.

Unlike at the doomed book event in Ayr, seven years
previously, I know what I'm getting into. The capacity
of the Skegness Embassy is 1,136 seats, and the audience
I'm heading towards consists of . . . well, yes, pretty much
1,136 *seats*. We've sold just about one hundred tickets out of
that eleven hundred, which – to save you doing the maths
in your head – is quite a long way short of sold out. I know
what it is going to feel like on that stage, because it's been
that sort of tour.

The same has already happened in Grimsby Auditorium, where by far the loudest noise was the gale howling
through the double doors at the back of the room, and
where I was outsold ten to one by a psychic. At the Liverpool Empire, the nearest audience members were so
far away that it would have made more sense for me to
write the show down and post it to them. Because of slow
sales at Middlesbrough Town Hall, the show was moved
from the actual hall into a crypt underneath the building where there were at least a few skeletons to bulk out
the numbers a bit. At the SECC in Glasgow, sales were
actually quite respectable, but still nowhere near enough

to be unembarrassing because the capacity of the venue would have made Lady Gaga herself wonder if she'd over-stretched.

It's bad tour planning by my producers, yes, and it's hubris on the part of my managers but, yet again, the buck stops with me. I always knew it was a big ask to fill these venues. And I knew, if I was honest, that it would be psychologically damaging to yell my show into the void of a sparsely populated Victorian mega-theatre, to hear the applause die away like very light rain on a summer's night, to have the invariably lovely front-of-house staff say consoling things like, 'Maybe they didn't advertise it very well,' or accidentally wounding things like, 'We had Jason Manford here and he was sold out in ten minutes.' I could have told myself that it would be hard to put on a brave face if this went on for thirty or forty nights consecutively. If I had been honest with myself; if I'd had the courage needed to access that honesty.

But honesty isn't what this profession is famed for. I was paid to make out everything was absolutely fine. And – as people kept pointing out to me – nobody had to know. All they had to know was that I was 'touring the big theatres'. 'Mark has just embarked on a sixty-date tour of major venues,' read a press release that I signed off around that time. The phrasing struck me as pretty fanciful, because it was normally people like Marco Polo who 'embark' on things, not comedians catching the train to Norwich. Still, as the tour wore on, it came to seem more and more

appropriate; what I had in common with the great circum-
navigators was that quite a few days would go by without
seeing a living soul.

My then tour producer Giles – a pragmatic man, with a
sense of humour forged in the tough world of live entertainment – made sure that I saw the funny side of all this
and it was with him that I hatched a plan for the Skegness
show. Once out there on the stage, I addressed the elephant
in the room, which was that we could have fitted quite a
lot of elephants into the room. Then I asked everyone in
the audience to join me on the stage. They all fitted without difficulty. I went down into the spacious auditorium
and – without needing to use a microphone – delivered
the show to them from there.

It was, as in Ayr, a moment of shared humanity; there
was a Blitz spirit about the whole thing. But it was not
what you'd call a success. It was an attempt at resistance by
a lone figure being swept away by the tide. It was the sort
of evening about which an audience member might say –
looking back, wondering if it had been a dream – 'That
poor guy, but fair play, what a good sport.' And at the start
of my thirties, with a new baby and a hefty mortgage, that
wasn't quite how I wanted to be seen.

The way I've phrased that probably tells its own story.
What was most upsetting to me wasn't really the financial
pressure that an unprofitable tour would put me under.
Most of the risk wasn't really mine, for a start; it was the

promoters'. Yes, the mortgage was a worry – as is any fiscal commitment, in a career as changeable as comedy – and, to make matters worse, we had builders renovating the place, which is one of the most stressful situations on this earth. The builder liked to be paid in cash, and, not being British, he was not in the habit of mincing his words. Every Friday I would receive a chilling text that said something like, 'Toilet seat is wrong shape, doorbell will not work, please transfer today £750.'

But it wasn't as if I was struggling the way some people struggle; the stress of a terrifyingly expensive refurb is the definition of a first-world problem. It wasn't necessarily that the under-attended gigs were even so bad to play. A decent comedian ought to be able to give a crowd a good time whether they *are* technically a 'crowd' or just a 'loosely spaced collection of people trying bravely to generate an atmosphere'. The real source of the pit-of-the-stomach feeling that followed me around the country had nothing to do with bills: it was to do with what was going on in my brain.

My issue was what they call a framing problem: not so much the situation, but how it would be *seen*. Even though we'd all agreed they would never know, they couldn't know – how these gigs would look to the other comedians out there, who were able to sell the tickets I couldn't. The people I saw as my competitors, who were tweeting things like, 'Hey, sorry to everyone who came tonight and couldn't get in – we're adding an extra show tomorrow night and we're talking to the theatre about adding a new wing in the next twenty-four hours, plus we are selling five-pound tickets to stand outside the building and laugh when you think a joke might have happened.'

I was not comparing myself with earlier versions of me, who would have been perfectly happy with where I'd got to. I wasn't even really comparing myself with potential versions of myself that I wanted to exist, which at least might have a constructive, aspirational aspect. Instead, I was comparing myself with comedians who were achieving what I wasn't and who I felt certain were therefore plugged into the mains of happiness in a way I was not. I wasn't trying to address the things that were wrong; I was focusing on the things that were right for other people.

Not everyone reading these words will have been guilty of this, but some of you will. When you look back on times you felt inadequate, you realise that a lot of what really hurt about it was that other people were seeing you suffer. That, in your head, your problem made you somehow inferior to them. That they were winning, and you were losing. We've already said it's dangerous to see life as a game with set objectives. But what happens in your brain if you start approaching it as a game you play *against other people*? I don't think it's much of a spoiler to say: the results are not good news.

At the end of a roughly fortnight-long stretch of these cheerful but demoralising shows, I found myself in a hotel in Albert Dock, Liverpool, one of a handful of establishments that have been a base for me in both good times and bad. In good times, I could afford it; in bad times, like this, I was there anyway because the accommodation had been booked with the assumption that it *would* be 'good times'. There was an unusual bath in my hotel room, stretched to fill the corner of the bathroom so that it had the rough dimensions of a hot tub. It was a luxurious bath by anyone's standards and on top of the minibar was a bottle of red wine. I'd become fond of wine in the past couple of years, but this is the first time that I remember having the idea that a few glasses would help to shut down the thoughts in my head, or at least slow them down. This was the first time that I used, albeit mentally, the phrase 'taking the edge off'. I opened and drank the wine, sitting in the bath, with my new smartphone in front of me. To an observer not given the context, I would have looked like a fairly successful person. I knew what I really was, though: a chancer posing as a successful person. And now, I told myself, everybody else was starting to catch up with the realisation.

I already knew that I wouldn't be back in the Liverpool Empire or the Town Hall at Middlesbrough, anytime soon. It isn't in the interests of venues to fill up with acts whose audiences are going to spend a total of thirteen pounds in the bar, especially when there are plenty of comics doing the rounds who are a viable proposition. And I knew also that a lot of the people who'd faithfully attended the shows wouldn't be back, either. Not that most of them hadn't enjoyed it, I thought. It was just that comedy relies on a sense of shared purpose and enjoyment and on experiencing something that other people aren't in on. That's why the comedy venues you remember most fondly are almost certainly rammed to the gills; the tickets are hard to come by, you feel special for having got in, and you begin the evening ready to laugh alongside the other people who have been equally smart. If you go and see a show and you're the only couple on a row meant for twenty-eight, not only will you come away remembering that you had to force out extra-loud laughs to keep the evening buoyant; you'll also be in no hurry to book next time around, because the image of the nine million empty seats will lodge in your brain.

The wheels were coming off, I told myself; everything I'd worked for was disintegrating. This both was and wasn't true. There were plenty of positives. I'd found a new publisher and my latest novel was doing all right – certainly better than the other two. I was still attracting *some* fans, I was still travelling around the country doing the thing I had set out to. When I look back at this period, the beginning of my inner civil war, I'm amazed at how cruel I was to myself, how unreasonable my expectations were. Why? Because those expectations were based on what other people were doing and how far I believed I was falling short of them. Once more, I should say I was not the first person, and will not be the last, to blunder into this way of thinking. But it so happened that I had chosen a really bad time to develop a series of neuroses.

It was the springtime of Facebook and Twitter which, for all their many upsides, quickly evolved from cute noticeboards for cat and baby pictures to giant, intimidating life scoreboards. *With* cat and baby pictures. If, like me, you had recently acquired a smartphone, you were holding in your hand the most powerful device ever created for drawing comparisons between yourself and other people. It was also very handy for crushing imaginary fruit and finding your way around a strange town. But you can guess which feature I gravitated towards.

One of the ways I tortured myself in that fake hot tub in Liverpool, and during many other late hotel nights, was by looking up people in my peer group who were doing better than I was. If I can excuse myself for this behaviour, I suppose I'd say that the entertainment industry does strong-arm you into doing this more than is healthy. An industry in which you are your own product – in which what you are selling is yourself; your own image, your own thoughts – can't help but be brutal in the way it pits one person against another.

In some areas of the entertainment game it's even worse: acting, for example. I remember being in the offices of a casting agent who was going through the CVs of actresses who were being considered for a pilot that I'd written (it never went anywhere, incidentally). The casting agent shuffled through the potential lead actresses – all of them people I thought would be pretty good, several of them I regarded as stars. She found a reason to dismiss each one, in the blink of an eye. 'She used to be a big thing, but she's gone off the boil a bit.' 'She's been piling on the pounds, for whatever reason.' 'I think she's generally seen as a bit too Irish, if you know what I mean.' Each time she rejected one of the candidates with a sentence like this, she would let the CV fall on to the desk, to be swallowed up in the slush pile. Some of them fell to the floor, like scrap paper, the hopeful faces nestling in a little bonfire of ambitions at her feet.

Competition is part of life. I had known this since I first made any sort of name for myself; after all, it had been positive for me. Winning a competition had given me my leg up into this career; going up against people was the way I had proved myself. But now, this same way of thinking had inevitably come back to torment me. Looking into the lives of others is as healthy an occupation as googling the phrase, 'How can I feel as dreadful as possible?' and I recommend it about the same amount. But it's so easily done. There was nothing to stop me and, with a bit of wine and a phone constantly lighting up with tailored reminders of other people's twenty-four-seven triumphs, there was more and more to keep me scrolling.

My particular poison was a comedian whose trajectory had been reasonably similar to mine. Around 2009 we had done a gig together in Kent – somewhere a bit more hospitable than Maidstone, but nonetheless not a place where there was a huge appetite for our style of comedy. We had done our sets to a modest response from an audience of about forty people, sharing a roughly four-hour round trip either side of our moment in the spotlight.

No more than six months after this car journey together, though, my fellow comedian had become very successful – luminously successful, a household name – and within a couple of years he had become the highest-grossing comedian in the world. This gentleman, with whom I'd shared an unprofitable evening near the coast in very recent memory, was now a bigger draw than Jerry Seinfeld. Anyone in my position would have a right to think, So, perhaps the problem is with me? I was never quite talented enough. I had wasted my potential. Something, in any case, separated me from this man, whose website, last time I checked it, has a picture of him grinning next to a globe – meant to represent his world tour – with the banner: '837,197 TICKETS SOLD; 242 SELL-OUT SHOWS'. His house has got a lake and a forty-piece orchestra in it and I only made one of those up (although I'm going by hearsay; he hasn't replied to my texts for a while).

There's a passage in David Nicholls's ten-trillion-selling novel *One Day*, which came out around that time. The protagonist, Dexter, is having to face up to the fact he isn't a big deal anymore. He's been a kind of MTV presenter/man-about-town, but those days are behind him, and now he's doing a traineeship in a sandwich shop.

The worst thing about it is the recognition, that flicker of pity that passes over a customer's face. To have had fame, even very minor fame, and to have lost it, got older and put on a little weight is a kind of living death.

These sentences came to haunt me. Of course, I was in a much more fortunate situation than this character. I didn't have to make sandwiches for anyone, I was still operative in my chosen career and I wasn't called Dexter. But the notion of the 'living death', even if it was exaggerated, became a mental peg to hang my decline on. The pity had started to creep into everyday conversations. I was already at the stage where relatives, at Christmas, would ask, 'So, any TV coming up?' with a tremor of anxiety in their voices on my behalf; the stage at which taxi drivers started to say, 'I haven't seen you on the box so much recently, mate, what have you been up to?'

It didn't have to be this hard, because I really didn't have to care this much what other people were up to, how their successes lined up alongside mine or what they thought of me.

'What people think of you is none of your business' – that's a wise saying credited to the actor Gary Oldman, although it was originally said by Mark Twain, and *he* probably got it from the back of a cereal packet or something. (You'll have spotted an emerging pattern; almost any piece of wisdom anyone's ever come up with either turns out to be slightly misquoted or has been nicked from someone else, which also teaches us a lesson about the value of fame.) This is one of those rules that would be great to live by, if it wasn't almost impossible. There has never been a time quite like this for finding out and caring about what others think. You don't even need to ask them anymore. They'll tell you.

One of the most common and most boring popular opinions in the modern world is that technology has 'ruined everything'. That, until sometime in the mid-nineties, we interacted flawlessly, articulating all our emotions, always making time for one another. Our children received a single wooden hoop for Christmas and were content with that. Instead of downloading entertainment on electronic devices, each street in a town took it in turns to put on a puppet show every night; instead of fiddling with apps during our commute, we passed the time by writing witty poems and reading them out to each other.

The people who speak most loudly about the ruinous effects of tech are normally pretty happy to get in a lift, for example, or use a car to get to work; you'll also rarely see them churning their own butter or reaching a holiday destination by lying on a homemade raft and waiting for the tide to take them to Greece. Sitting behind your newspaper tutting at the progress of machines is no more meaningful an exercise than standing on the beach shaking your fist at the sea as it advances towards you. Once we had computers, we had to have the internet one day; once we had the connectivity that the internet brings, social media was inevitable; once social media became a thing, it refined itself more and more until we were all endlessly interacting in real time. You can lament this as much as you want, but the benefits to us are huge.

Tools like Wikipedia and YouTube and Twitter allow us to share knowledge or ideas or art with an ease no generation has ever experienced before, opening up the wonders of our civilisation to millions of people who would have been locked out of them in times gone by. Facebook, WhatsApp and Instagram keep us in more constant contact with friends and loved ones than we could have dreamed of growing up. It is in our hands to all but end human loneliness, to create giant networks of like-minded humans, to tackle our global problems together. And a lot of that *has* been achieved by social media, from the #MeToo movement to the smaller life-enhancing connections that we don't see, but which are being made every day.

Of course, these platforms also have the potential to do great harm and they need to be more responsibly run, and in time their algorithms will become so advanced that our own laptops will learn how to kill us in our sleep. But it's no use talking as if 'the internet' somehow stole our brains or our humanity, and if you talk for any length of time to a person who says things like that, you'll very often find that they also think there hasn't been any decent music since the Bay City Rollers and that they 'tend to give foreign food a miss'.

What the internet *has* undeniably done to our minds, though, is to make us feel as if everything we do is part of a beauty contest. The currency of 'likes' means that you can get an instant reading on the popularity of your selfie or smartarse remark. There are plenty of people whose entire livelihoods rely on those figures and who use all sorts of tactics to boost them, making them appear at a glance as if their every utterance is many hundreds of times more worthwhile than yours. There are influencers who are earning more money for posting five minutes of video a week than you get for working in a primary school for a year. And they're only nineteen and don't have any living expenses because brands send them beds to sleep on, plane tickets to Dubai for their holidays, luxury dog food for their dogs and new dogs when they're tired of their current ones.

Even within your own friendship circles, every day on Facebook brings a cute picture of a family day out, 'I LOVE MUM' on a piece of pottery, which you read while you are cleaning sick off a cardigan. Or a status update which is just a photo of a couple on a balcony in Costa Rica, garlanded with dozens of heart-strewn comments, just as your dating app is reminding you that it's 2,600 days since you 'got out there'. Or there's the genre of post that doesn't even supply any detail, but just cryptically hints at someone feeling and doing better than you – 'Can't say anything yet, guys, but just had some news which has blown my mind!' – so that you don't even have the luxury of knowing in what way you're failing by comparison; you just know that you are.

In short, you don't need to be a performer, or in any kind of cut-throat business, to be drawn into competitiveness in the twenty-first century: life itself has been made into a competition.

All of us have been on the internet long enough to know how this works. And, if you speak to a friend who is down because they feel they are losing the competition, you know exactly what to say. You point out that when we're unhappy, the world can easily seem like a massive carnival; one which we can only see through our windows, when we can hear all the joyous noise made by others. We know objectively that this carnival doesn't really exist. Very few people are waking up in the morning and waving cheerleader pompoms in the air. Even people who are – broadly speaking – happy and fulfilled have a daily stream of baggage to contend with, because life is not gentle with anyone, not for long; it's full of small upsets and battles even for the shiniest personalities. It's never been true that 'everyone else is having a good time'. You just feel like they are, because you aren't. 'You're doing much better than you're making out,' you say to your discouraged friend. 'You're being much too hard on yourself. There's nothing that special about Callum; he just got lucky with that swan thing going viral.'

A cruel thing about being locked inside our own brains in the way we are, though, is that it's very difficult to treat ourselves with the same kindness we'd extend to others. It is hard to step outside ourselves and put an arm around our own shoulder. Even when we're not living to try to satisfy other people, or to achieve some far-fetched goal, we set ourselves years back; even when we're just getting on with the day-to-day we instinctively inflate the achievements of others and pour cold water on our own.

To question yourself, to hold yourself to standards – these are good qualities, the marks of a person with humility. You *want* to be that guy. A lot of life's tough emotional currents are the price of having an honest relationship with your own brain and your own fallibility; for example, I'm prepared to be honest about the fact I didn't spell 'fallibility' correctly at the first attempt. It's a heavy price to pay and, when the bill comes, you sometimes need someone to split it with you.

And I did still think that I had that backup. After all, I still had a manager. She didn't know how deeply I had started to doubt myself, but it was in her interests for me to find a way out of it. That was what I told myself. What I failed to appreciate was that I'd fallen so far in her estimation that her 'interests' no longer included me at all.

One afternoon, on the train to a show, I received an email. Well, she did have a plan, it turned out. It was for me to leave the agency. The email was two lines long. I felt numb, then angry, and then finally, of course, mortified and empty. And by the time all these stages had played out, I was getting off the train, and it was time to go on stage again and act like everything was great.

We had been working together for just under a decade – I was one of her oldest clients, and had stuck with the agency when it went through a very difficult period. Now it turned out we had spoken face-to-face for the last time ever, except for a very awkward pass-in-the-street moment about a year later, where we both mouthed a 'hello', like exes, and went our separate ways into the night. It was not the most wounding or inexplicable rejection in store for me, the most harrowing ghosting. But it was plenty to be dealing with for now.

To be in someone's life for nearly ten years and then to be told that you're not needed anymore is a smack in the mouth, and even when it comes from someone you have been working with, the feelings are pretty similar to getting dumped. You are obviously not good enough; maybe they've been thinking this for months. Maybe you should have taken it more seriously when, for your birthday, they bought you six books about how to bring snoring under control. At least with a relationship, though, there's often not an immediate replacement – or at least the dumper has the decency to *pretend* there isn't. If you're chucked by your manager, however, you only have to look on the website and find the twenty-five people she's still with.

Maybe the universe is doing this for a reason, I tried to think; maybe it was always time to move on, and this is just forcing my hand. I've never been fond of the notion 'everything happens for a reason', as it makes an indiffer-ent, chaotic universe sound like a kindly old grandfather. I don't think I'd want to say it to someone who'd just seen their brother fall into the Grand Canyon. But there's a virtue in reading setbacks – even pretty crushing ones, like this – as an incentive to try new things. When I'd got a little bit of courage back, and picked myself off the floor, I tried to think of it this way.

I got a meeting with a potential new manager, someone I'd always admired, someone who I thought would be perfect to reboot my career. 'You are not a failure; you are a success waiting to happen all over again,' I lectured myself. It isn't easy, when things have been going against you, to say this sort of stuff in your head; it's harder still to say it out loud, to someone you're trying to impress. I had to prove I wasn't finished and that meant I first had to prove it to *myself*. I downloaded my own profile from Chortle, the online comedy encyclopaedia, and for the final few minutes of the journey to the meeting I stared at it, trying to absorb all the good stuff I'd done, trying to let that feeling seep into my skin, until I noticed that the couple next to me could see what I was up to.

The meeting seemed to go well. The high-ranking manager asked me about some of my decisions and what I thought I should have done differently; where I felt things had gone wrong. We agreed on various moves we could try to get things going again, new tactics. She expressed the hope that we might be able to 'do something together'.

I left, feeling a bit less like a sodden mattress someone had left outside a flat with the note: 'FREE STUFF, PLEASE TAKE'.

But when the follow-up phone call came, it was bad news. 'I don't think I'm going to be able to do anything for you,' said the woman I'd hoped would be my new manager. It was going to be pretty tough for me, she went on, after 'everything that had already happened'. The phrase made it sound as if I'd been convicted of a series of murders rather than having been in a series of TV shows that didn't work out. 'I can't really see you having the career you want,' she summarised, sounding genuinely apologetic. I thanked her. I hung up the phone. I was crying and I hoped she hadn't been able to tell.

I'd been rejected by two people I respected, in quick succession. Who were the comedians they wanted, instead of me? Who were the people now having what I'd hoped would be my career?

Once more, the answers were easily available. All I had to do was get my phone out once again. Scroll masochistically through the Twitter boasts, browse the grinning faces of the frightening new talents whose headshots now graced the agency site. In what felt like a slightly Stalinist manoeuvre, I had already been deleted from the site *by the time I read the email asking me to leave*. I told myself that all these bright new successors had hit upon something I hadn't; had avoided the sort of mistakes that had sent me sprawling. In darker moments, I even imagined that they had avoided those mistakes by studying mine; that I'd become a cautionary tale for aspiring entertainers, that they laughed about me backstage. Maybe, I told myself, 'doing a Watson' was a popular shorthand for 'starting really promisingly, then going off the rails'. Like a jilted lover, I fantasised about the new favourites of my former manager, sitting in the bars we used to go to, CCing each other into tedious email chains just like we used to CC each other.

Of course, the thing with easily available answers is that they're often wrong. Nobody had 'taken my career instead of me' and nobody could: that's what the *actual* answer was. Just as nobody can live anyone's life for them or decide better than any of us how it should be done, no one can somehow steal the life or career we were meant to have had.

There are, for sure, times in life when it feels as if someone's good fortune comes directly at your expense. You are sitting waiting to do a job interview and they come out of the room with a glass of champagne and say, 'Thank you so much, I'm buzzing, I can't wait to get started!' You put your hand up twelve times at a Q&A with your favourite TV personality, bursting with a question that shows such detailed knowledge of the celeb's upbringing that they are certain to marry you the instant you ask it, but each time the moderator goes for someone else, then says, 'I'm afraid we have to end here' after the *bastard* next to you had done the cheat's trick of going, 'I've actually got two questions.'

You are on that dating show where you have to impress a crowd of women who turn their lights off; when you come out with your juggling clubs, the lights black out as if there's been a power outage and then the contestant after you pulls out a flamenco guitar and several of the women faint clean away with desire. Of course, when you see these things (or are rejected in more serious ways) it's pretty hard not to feel that something has been taken from you, by someone who was either luckier or prettier or in some way better.

But nothing has been taken, really. Because that other person is completely different and a million factors determine what happens to them, and almost all of those have nothing to do with you. That other person is not – much as we all sometimes see people this way – a bit-part character in the TV series of your life. They are starring in their own series. They are not something which is 'happening to you'. They're just out there, a separate set of molecules, living a separate life. Looking at someone else and thinking, That should have been me, makes no more sense really than seeing a video of an elephant picking up a log with its trunk and thinking, *That* should have been me. You could only ever have been yourself; you could not have been the elephant.

Anyway, success – like happiness, like everything you want – is not a chemical element of which the world contains a finite amount. It isn't a drink everyone is simultaneously trying to get at with long straws. Someone else's success doesn't diminish yours. This is an important thing to remember, especially if you're in a job as competitive and as full of universal lust for success as entertainment: almost every day you'll hear of something big happening for one of your contemporaries and, if you allow every one of those to feel as if it was something that they won *instead of you*, you will be almost constantly exhausted.

But at the time of my life that we're now coming to, I didn't understand that at all. And so, even though things were starting to unravel, there were worse times ahead. When you have allowed your own mind to become the enemy, when your own personality is a room you can't live in anymore, there are always worse times ahead.

'Living death' is a powerful phrase, but it shouldn't really be used to describe the feeling of a taxi driver expressing concern for your career or Deborah grabbing a work opportunity that you should have had, even though her personality is so wafer-thin she describes eating a cinnamon bun as 'being a bit naughty'. It can mean something much more fundamental and frightening: it can be a point at which you don't really recognise, let alone like, the person you are. It is a bad place. I went there; I hope you don't have to.

6

HE SEEMS LIKE HE'S DOING OK

There is a dickhead on stage. He's everything you hate about watching comedy in a club. Well, not *everything* perhaps. He hasn't tried to impress the guys on their stag night by telling you that your shirt makes you look like you're gay; he hasn't done a joke about the number of virgins supposedly promised to Islamic suicide bombers, which – if it were possible to make a scientific study – would be the subject most often and most tediously visited by substandard comedians in that period. (It was borderline racist as a trope even when it was most fashionable and, besides, it's hardly topical anymore, but you'd be amazed how long some comedians will cling on to a piece of material. I remember several years into my career seeing a veteran comic do a gag about the fire at Windsor Castle, which had happened in 1992. It was so long ago that he had to explain the joke by saying, '. . . because, remember, there was a fire there' afterwards. He's probably still performing it.)

No, the comedian is not an aggressive sort, not a bully, but he is a very, very uncomfortable watch tonight, all the same. He hesitates, begins punchlines that he doesn't satisfactorily finish. He mentions several times that he doesn't think he's doing as well as the previous comedians on the bill, which is true but, of course, becomes all the more true the more he says it. He seems to have been thoroughly psyched out by the task of headlining the show. And he's right, everyone else has been great so far, but it's not as if this is a competition. Quite the opposite: they're all on the same team, both performers and audience, because this is a charity night. It's being held in support of a mental health charity and in memory of a local man who tragically died by suicide. There is no sense that anyone in the audience is here to make trouble. They just want to have a good time. They were *having* a good time, until this unfortunate started stumbling through his set in front of them.

It isn't as if he's a newcomer, out of his depth in this place – the main comedy venue in Brighton but still a pretty unintimidating size. The guy has been on TV a fair few times; you saw him once and you thought he was OK. He's even been on this stage more than once before. Your friend's mum, who loves comedy and talks about Radio 4 figures as if they were Hollywood icons, came to see him on tour here a couple of years ago and she said he was not only funny, but a very nice chap who stayed behind afterwards to sign her CDs. She'd been happy to hear he was married, with a child, not like some of these slightly more 'racy' entertainers – 'racy' being the word your friend's mum uses for anything with spicier language or content than *Dad's Army*.

What happened to *that* man? you wonder. He certainly isn't here tonight. The guy who's here really shouldn't still be on the stage. And he knows it.

This is actually the most common kind of death you can see in a comedy club: death by mutual mortification. It's one of the most underestimated factors in the deaths-of-comedians statistics every year. People who don't spend a lot of time in comedy venues, whose idea of one is based either on a confrontational scene in an American drama or on a hazy recollection of a bad night out in Croydon in 1995, always picture comedians like gladiators before an emperor, hoping for their lives to be spared, pleading for the uplift of a thumb. It's because of this idea that a lot of comedy *is* so aggressive; plenty of acts seem to come from the starting point that the gig is something to be survived, something to plough through while sustaining as little damage as possible. But most audiences are, in fact, not like that. After all, they have come out hoping to enjoy themselves. When most people watch a comedian walk on the stage, their primary emotion is hope; hope that things are going to go well. They know that watching a comedian suffer will feel like suffering themselves. Apart from some really wrong-headed people, everyone in a comedy night wants the same thing: for it to be fun. That huge laugh when the first big joke lands is a laugh of shared relief and gratitude.

That's why it's such a terrible experience to see this once popular act floundering in front of everyone. And, wait, he isn't done yet. Abandoning his attempts to make you laugh, he adopts an earnest tone. He says that mental health is really important and urges everyone not to kill themselves. It is meant to strike a serious note, in keeping with the wider aims of the evening. But it comes out sounding fatuous, as if the guy is trying to find an irreverent angle on the charity's serious mission. Nobody in the audience is actively hostile, but there is a real discomfort in the room now and, when the comedian leaves the stage to a smattering of applause, everyone is pretty grateful to see him go.

The MC does a courteous job – 'Put your hands together for Mark Watson!' He then completes the formalities, acknowledging all the acts, reminding everyone of what a good cause this is. I am in the dressing room, right behind the stage, and I can hear all this, but it isn't really going in; I am sobbing, and there's a sort of rushing noise in my ears, like the sound of a panic attack distilled.

Films and TV, pub gossip, language itself lead us to see mental health challenges, addictions, damaging behavioural patterns in quite simplistic terms. A guy who appears on stage drunk is a 'booze hound' or has 'always had a problem with it'. A woman who shuts herself in her room for four weeks, because she can't get out of bed, is 'having a nervous breakdown'. A man who hits the age of fifty and gets freaked out by the idea that more than half his life is behind him and starts to travel compulsively, or seeks out a new relationship, is undergoing 'a midlife crisis'. We are keen on simple, shorthand explanations for other people's behaviour. It's a lot less time-consuming than delving into the details and, well, we're all short of time.

If you had seen me that night in Brighton, you would have pretty quickly come to the conclusion that I was drunk on stage and you would have been right. And if you'd chatted to me for ten minutes the night before or the night after, you'd have come away thinking that I was pretty depressed. You would have been right about that, too. But you'd be seeing the symptoms, not the causes.

People do not, in general, suddenly 'lose it' – 'it' being their faith in what they're doing on this earth and their belief in their ability to do it successfully. It might look that way from the outside, but inside it's a process that runs for weeks, months or years. By the time they start to exhibit those outward signs that are apparent to everyone – the erratic performances, the one-too-many drinks, the sudden screaming fit outside Cardiff Central station, to take an entirely random example – the inner decay has been happening for a long time. Being in a bad mental health situation is a bit like being a building with serious structural difficulties. All the passers-by on the street witness is the moment the edifice finally falls down, ideally caught on camera and put online for massive amounts of clicks. But the rot has been spreading below the surface for a long time. The warning signs have been there all along. (If only you'd listened to your dad when he took a look around and said, 'This seems a bit of a risk to me,' but the thing is, he also said that about all the other twenty-four houses you looked around.)

By 2013, ten years after I began comedy in earnest, I was a house about to collapse. I had let so much of myself be whittled away and I had replaced each mental wall with mental plasterboard. But even people standing very, very close didn't know how near the whole thing was to falling over. We're all interested in the moment itself; the shattering of glass. We're not so good at looking for the signs beforehand. I wasn't even looking for them myself. Sometimes, even if you're in the house, you don't know until it's too late.

I've told you about the way that I sabotaged myself by comparing my life and career to others', positioning everything as a game and convincing myself that I was losing that game more and more heavily. What would have been a good approach at this point was to ask myself *why* I was so intent on what psychologists would call these 'negative narratives'. Why was I telling myself this story which could only make me feel bad?

I needed to work on ways to stop myself playing the game at all. What I did instead was to play harder, more frantically, even though everyone else had gone home and the only remaining 'opponents' were the areas of my life I was neglecting. These included my friendships and my family life. I had a child now, with another one on the way, and I was bluffing my way through the dads' events – the picnics with kids on our laps, the toddler talk – as if I didn't feel permanently on the verge of a collapse. I was still travelling around a lot, trying to hold on to what audience I retained, accepting any and every gig: my non-appearance at weddings and parties was almost accepted as a given. This brought the benefit that people I knew well couldn't see how poorly I was holding together the charade of being an upbeat and successful thirty-something. In fact, being a comedian, in perpetual motion, working late nights and in unpredictable parts of the country, always rushing out of the door, never quite being able to hold a full-length phone conversation – all of this was excellent camouflage for a human falling apart.

Yes, he seems like he's doing OK, well-wishers would think; *he's just so busy all the time.* People a little closer to me often expressed concern that I was 'pushing myself too hard', 'taking too much on', and worried that I would suffer some sort of burnout. It was true that I was burning the candle at both ends. I was also then going to the shop for another candle and burning it on the walk home. It was true that this way of living was punishing and that, every time I was close to getting on top of it, I undermined myself by cramming in still more things. But it wasn't that I'd got addicted to working too much and was imploding as a result, even though that was a reasonable assumption for people to make. It was more the other way around: I was overfilling my life *because* I was on the brink of disintegration and didn't know how else to address it.

My marriage was going pretty badly and I had had an affair, which ended – with enormous pain caused to two different people – not long after the birth of our second child. Of course, it doesn't feel good to write this down. It didn't feel good to cause lasting damage to people in the way I did. There isn't anything I can say to excuse my behaviour and there's almost nothing I will ever be able to do to atone for my actions, although I've tried in various ways.

A couples therapist would later tell me that I was 'acting out' – rather than try to address what wasn't working in my life, I was searching for something better, a parallel universe, an alternative life. I was digging myself deeper into that trap and my anxiety levels were the highest they had ever been. At night I would lie in brittle, patchy sleep and wake up at 4am with my insides churning, clammy with sweat, unable to lie still. Those pulse-racing nights, staring out at the dark, with the wails of children in the house and with every kind of self-inflicted problem swilling around my stomach, were the longest of my life, and yet they were also over much too quickly: when you are dreading the daybreak, the night has a way of just draining out of the sky.

Work remained my hiding place and, as hiding places go, it was not going to protect me forever; I could hear the footsteps of the search party getting close. There are times in life when it's completely legitimate to throw yourself into work; to make it your main focus and source of energy. I've always considered myself lucky, in fact, to have things I care about enough that I *can* find that energy in them: my books, my gigs, my internationally acclaimed choral work. But even if you love it, work can't be the only thing that you plough your brain and soul into. That will only sustain you as long as things are going well. And, as I think we've established by now, quite a lot of the time in life things *won't* go as well as you'd like.

I had found a new manager, but it was slow going trying to get TV people interested in me again, and I didn't know how I could tell people that without feeling even more of a failure, and a public one. I was trying to broaden my range of career options, so that I'd be relying less on the bloody arena of stand-up; but, unfortunately, the main alternative route to success was writing and, in terms of security, that's like saying, 'This house of cards is a bit precarious; I know, I'll go and live in that one made of Rice Krispies.'

I lost one particular, treasured project that left me feeling bereft – more so than I would have been if I'd been living in a more psychologically healthy way. It was a TV adaptation of my novel *Eleven*, the only book that had really managed to make an impact on the general public. I was writing the adaptation myself: if it got the green light, my life would change drastically in the key fields of money, self-esteem, and 'not having a TV show based on my novel'.

There were a lot of hoops to jump through before the show could get made, of course. And the trouble is, some of these hoops are invisible, in the sense that you don't know what TV people are looking for because they don't really know themselves (as the *Peep Show* visionary showed us earlier). Others are so difficult to vault through that they might as well be on fire and you might as well be a horse, as in the circuses of old, before people started saying, 'Hang on, I definitely don't think we should be doing this.' But I'd come through quite a few of these hoops already, and was now at the stage where I got to meet an actual commissioner.

The commissioner in whose hands my future rested was about my age, but I had the sense that he'd looked after himself quite a lot better over those same years; sitting across the table from him, I felt that I gave off an air of desperation. He wore shoes that were more expensive than all the clothes in my wardrobe put together, and the sort of tailored shirt you see advertised in Sunday broadsheets' glossy magazines. He drank sparkling water in the meeting, which meant I had to, too; I doubted he'd had more than three beers in his life. He looked like he spent up to a quarter of his time in wellness retreats and, if not fully vegan, had significantly reduced his meat intake over the past couple of years because 'you start to realise your body doesn't need it'. I felt diminished by the sheer health and wellness of the man and by the authority he had, at the press of a button, to change the course of my life. But we seemed to get on. I made him laugh; he really seemed to believe in my book as a possible TV hit, even in 'this difficult climate', which is a phrase commissioners use in every meeting regardless of what is happening in the world, just to cover themselves if they have to let you down. He had even read the novel and had ideas about it, something which I found disproportionately thrilling because most people in his role are loath to read anything longer than a text message and look at a three-hundred-page novel as if they're being asked to wade through the *Chronicles of King Arthur* on the original parchment. The meeting didn't conclude with confetti dropping down from the ceiling and an official presenting me with an oversized novelty cheque, but it had gone as well as I could have hoped.

It was three months before the email arrived. In five seconds, I thought, I would see either 'I'm delighted to let you know that . . .' – the words I had spent literally years dreaming of reading – or the familiar 'I'm sorry to be the bearer of bad news'. Somehow, though, it was neither. The news was that my commissioner was leaving his post. In fact, he was leaving the commissioning business altogether. Why? He'd decided to move close to the sea to pursue his secret ambition of writing young adult fiction. That's right: the person I'd pinned my hopes upon to revive my writing dreams had decided to concentrate on his own writing dreams instead. By the sea.

Like that, it was over. He did say – at the foot of what was, obviously, a group email – that all existing projects would be passed into the 'extremely capable hands' of whoever ended up being promoted into his position, but I knew what that meant. A project passed to a new commissioner has as much chance of surviving intact as a thimble of water being passed to someone on a bouncy castle. The first thing the new incumbent does is stamp his or her own authority on the position and 'pass' your project straight into the bin. The message confirming the binning arrived within the week.

There are plenty more stories like this. There was a meeting with a powerful BBC guy who was considering one of my comedy-drama ideas. He said that he liked the idea but he wasn't sure I was the right person for the channel; wasn't sure I understood the 'tone' the viewers were after. He suggested that I go away and watch a few of the hits they'd had recently: for example, he said, something called *A Child's Christmases in Wales*.

'But . . . *I* wrote that,' I pointed out, quietly. There was a bit of a pause.

'Right,' said the man in charge of the channel, 'I probably should have known that.' A secretary soon came in to tell him it was time to meet someone else and I was shown the exit. He never answered another one of my emails.

Incidents such as this might have been enough to put a person with a healthy perspective off the whole idea of TV. But I didn't have that perspective anymore. It had been sent off the rails by the mental habits I've already talked about: the thirst for success – of any kind – and the perception that other people had that success. I wanted someone to want me. If that's your mentality in the world of entertainment, you're going to end up being seen as disposable goods. And from then on, you are heading for the saddest three words in the game: *Celebrity Storage Hunters*.

When I appeared on this show, I had to bid on mystery items in storage units, winning money for charity if they turned out to be valuable. I bid on what proved to be parts of a Harley-Davidson motorbike and turned a healthy profit. They then brought out a fully assembled bike and asked me to get on it with an 'instructor', who was just a guy with a beard they'd likely recruited at some seventies hard-rock reunion gig.

The man gave me some extremely cursory instructions like, 'This is your clutch, essentially, and this is your brake' but, as I couldn't actually drive any sort of vehicle, this wasn't very helpful. Suddenly, he said, 'Right, I'm handing over to you.'

I tried to explain that I hadn't signed up for this, that I'd been told we were just posing on the bike and taking a brief spin for a bit of filler between the longer chunks of filler that were the show itself, but nobody was listening. I was now in charge of the bike and shouting in fear. I could hear the instructor, perched behind me, yelling, 'No, no, no,' as we zoomed towards one of the garages. We smashed into the wall and I blacked out briefly.

When I came around, someone asked me to confirm verbally that the show had no responsibility for my accident, and unfortunately I did. Surprising as it may sound, when the episode went to air, this incident was nowhere to be seen. Unwisely, I tweeted something to that effect and offers from TV started to thin out a bit – almost as if *I* had been the one who put someone on a bike and let them go head-first into a garage. All those people stayed in their jobs, I expect. Knowing the industry as I do, it wouldn't amaze me if one of them had won a BAFTA for 'Most Conscientious Avoidance of Head Injuries on a TV Set'.

But the point is that these things happen to everyone in a game like this and we all know it and, in a better frame of mind, a person like me would laugh it off. In the frame of mind of 2016 Mark Watson, however, everything was further proof of failure and of worse times ahead.

For periods of my life, as I've said, my brain and I have not felt as if we were on the same team. By the middle of the last decade, we were actively enemies to one another. If you've ever been in an unhappy flat-share, you'll know what it's like to see someone every day who undermines your sense of wellbeing. Imagine having that toxic influence living not in your spare room, but in your own head. It starts to get pretty claustrophobic in there. That's where I was, at this point in life. And it wasn't as if I had other accommodation options. There is only one way of moving out of your brain, and I was starting to find it more tempting.

How can you and your brain become separate entities? We think of our brains as containing our whole selves, all our personality. But anyone with experience of poor mental health will tell you that it's more than possible for your sense of self and your conscious brain to go different ways. You keep walking around doing tasks, going from Monday to Friday, following the routines that are meant to make up a life. But your own internal monologue speaks against you. It only gives you the most negative reading of what's happening. It latches on to any piece of evidence that supports the idea you're no use and quietly discards anything that speaks in your favour. It is starting to bring you down from the inside. When you are in a mentally unwell frame of mind, your brain is just like that: a frame. You can only see the facts that your inner director wants you to see; hear the story they want you to hear. If that story is that you're unlovable, finished in your career and not the person that you set out to be, it's very hard to escape the cold feelings that those messages bring.

We don't have the option of an 'off' switch and the best that many of us can do is to turn the volume down. There are lots of ways of trying to 'take the edge off' life and almost all of them have upsides, yet there is a lot of judgemental nonsense talked about how we may choose to do this. There are people who'll make out that everyone who fanatically supports a football team or writes *Doctor Who* fan fiction, for example, is doing it because they're incapable of committing to anything more 'adult' or substantial; that anyone who enjoys a few drinks or another recreational drug is some tragic figure in a piano bar in a black-and-white movie; that anyone who watches a frothy movie or reads an airport page-turner is empty-headed. These people are merely short of imagination or empathy. The ability to immerse yourself in the fictional universe of a TV show, or emotionally pin yourself to the fortunes of a sports team, goes hand in hand with having a range of interests outside your immediate surroundings. In short, you should be suspicious of people who *don't* have their poisons. We're not meant to live in our brains absolutely every minute of every day.

But it's also true that if you go too far into alternative mental spaces – if you start to become so happy in them that you never want to come back – that *is* bad news. Going on holiday is meant to be a fun glimpse of a different reality, an escape; if you are crushed with misery at the idea that you have to come home, though, you need to ask yourself whether you should address what's wrong *with* home rather than just saving up to get away from it again in another fifty weeks. Likewise: if you're scared of what is waiting for you back in your brain once the drink wears off or the film is over, the solution is not another drink.

'Wherever you go, there you are' is a phrase you'll find in self-help a lot: in fact it was the title of an influential book that became one of the pillars of mindfulness. It's one of these phrases that you instinctively rebel against because it sounds about as worthwhile as saying, 'When you get in your car, you are sitting in your car.' But it does contain a useful, inescapable truth. No matter how many barriers you put between yourself and your own brain, it *is* still your brain and you have to live with it. If you're finding that almost impossible to bear, you have to work out sooner or later what you're going to do about that.

I've been reasonably transparent about the fact that I really, really enjoy wine and I am pretty comfortable acknowledging it as one of my most loyal companions. Wine to me is as delicious as cheese seems to be to everyone except me, or chocolate is to housewives in the imaginations of male ad execs. It's always been a sensory pleasure more than a purely psychological one. All the same, during my thirties I started to notice that the insulating effect of drinking was more than just something I liked to experience occasionally. It was something I began to want all the time. Being tipsy Mark Watson was much smoother and more enjoyable than being the regular edition. I became adept at finding justifications for having a drink in any given situation. Someone's birthday; someone's last day before starting a new job; the anniversary of someone's uncle's christening . . . let's raise a glass! It worked with times of

the year, too. 'Ooh, it's cold: let's have a winter warmer.'
'It's a lovely summer's day: what about a refreshing white
wine?' Before you know it, it's: 'Ah, springtime! There's a
newborn lamb! LET'S HAVE A VODKA.'

This wouldn't have been so much to worry about if I
had been happy; comfortable in the skin of the person I
returned to when the drinking sessions were over. But, of
course, I was not; those sessions were like a series of mini
day trips away from my actual life. That life had become
something I didn't feel equal to. The comedowns were
becoming more and more severe: not because of hang-
overs or the brittle, morning-after paranoia that can kick
in when you check the texts you've sent without receiving
a reply, but because of a much more fundamental problem.
I was now enjoying the warm, phantom world of booze
much more than the reality I was coming back to. The
knock-on effect of this was predictable enough: I started
spending more and more time in booze world and less and
less on my real responsibilities and relationships.

Even when physically present in my everyday life, part
of me was thinking about the next time I could get away
from it, turn off my main brain, live in the foam insula-
tion of my evening mind. I had never been one of these
miserable drinkers you hear about, who look at the bottle
and think, I don't even want this, I've just got to. No, my
thing was more looking at the bottle and thinking, Yum,
I shall enjoy drinking what's in there. But now, the heady
escape of alcohol had taken on a slightly joyless aspect. The

wish to be transported away from my problems needed fuelling as a matter of urgency. A desolate station pub, the sort with a carpet and *Bargain Hunt* playing on the big TV because they haven't paid the subscription fee for Sky Sports, would do as well as a party full of friends. It wasn't so much about the fun of going somewhere else; it was just about the relief of being there.

One Hollywood cliché of addiction that does stand up is that, before long, you need to get more of whatever it is that works in order for it to have the same effect. And that was the sort of impulse that would occasionally lead to me massively overdoing it before a gig, just to try to feel all right. Which in turn led to me being too drunk to think of funny words and put them into the correct order and eventually to me leaving the stage to the sort of applause that suggested I would be better off gigging closer still to the south coast, i.e., in the sea.

But that disastrously pitched gig was only a micro-crisis compared with the omni-crisis of a life I had got myself into. I had started to lose interest in making things better for myself. The corollary of that feeling is that you believe everyone else has lost interest in you, too. People use the phrase 'dying a little bit inside' very casually, but – as with the phrase 'living death' – it can have a very specific, and alarming, meaning. If you were in charge of a child or a pet and you ceased caring about their wellbeing, wheth-er anything happened to them, anyone would see that it would be a disaster. Plenty of us, though, reach a point in our lives where we're treating our own selves with similar neglect. This was the point that I had reached and it felt simultaneously frightening and oddly passive. I had gone past the 4am panics, walking the emotional high-wire. Or, I was still on the wire, but hardly bothering to look at my feet, hardly interested in the question of whether there was going to be a fall.

In a novel I published in 2020, called *Contacts*, a man in his late thirties gets pretty much to this point. He sends a text to his whole phone book – to everybody in his contacts list – telling them that he's going to end his life. Then he gets on a sleeper train and puts the phone on to flight mode so he can't see any of the replies. The novel goes through the night as the people in James's life try to talk him out of what he's threatening to do, without actually being able to reach him. Thank you, yes, it *is* quite an appealing hook; you can still find it in bookshops.

I never sent a message like James's; I never shut my phone off for one dramatic night – but I had become that person, and on at least one occasion I was a couple of text exchanges away from ending things. I knew that my life insurance policy would pay out handsomely if something happened to me, and that the savings and assets I'd accumulated would sort my children out at least for a good while. That seemed much more of a proposition than anything I had to offer them while I remained around. People could barely reach me anymore. I didn't really want them to. I had put the book of my own life down. I didn't care if it continued or not.

You will often hear it said that we're all basically on our own, have to be responsible for our own survival. It's an alarmingly prevalent idea within certain areas of what is supposed to be the self-help industry. *'The only one who can help you is yourself.'* *'If you want something done properly, do it yourself.'* *'You have to be your own best friend.'* *'If you don't like yourself, who will?'* The internet – so, in other words, the world – is teeming with supposed experts on wellness whose message essentially boils down to this: work out what you want to get, set it as a goal and go headlong towards it, whatever the collateral damage. The misleading idea is that if you're not happy with your life you ought to see that as a rectifiable failure of some kind.

Just as life is not a game you win or lose, it isn't something you have to tackle on your own. It's a team effort. We live in public. People talk a lot of bollocks about 'tribes' and our primal instincts; there are good reasons why we've developed beyond them – such as the fact that living in a house is noticeably better than living in a cave and spreading human waste to mark our territory is much less workable as a system than just having separate door numbers.

But one thing we have lost track of a bit, over the centuries, is our need to work as communities. Our way of ordering society into little family units, each living in a small box, has robbed us of the sense that we're part of one big collective. (If you've had small children and heard the phrase, 'It takes a village to raise a child', you will almost certainly also have had the experience of wrestling your kid into a buggy next to Argos, and, as the child flails its little fists in your face, thinking, Where the fuck is this village I was promised?) We live our lives now like a game show, not a collective effort.

Life is about opening yourself up to being part of a team, not walking into the dark by yourself. It was a lesson I desperately needed to learn, but one I was resistant to hearing. I mentioned earlier the idea that 'what other people think of you is none of your business'. Like so many other well-meaning aphorisms, it is actually only half true. Yes, by all means tune out the criticism or the judgemental talk of people with nothing invested in you. But don't bar the door so firmly that it can't be opened by the people who actually matter. What some people thought of me was *absolutely* my business. Hearing their voices would help me survive. Like the people trying to text James in my novel, though, they could not – in that moment – reach me. I needed to open myself up to them. For that, my brain needed fresh air, a new start.

A MARATHON, NOT A SPRINT
(OR: WHAT ENDURANCE EVENTS TAUGHT ME ABOUT THE WAY TO LIVE, 2017–18) (I'M SORRY, YES, THERE'S LITTLE WORSE THAN SOMEONE BANGING ON ABOUT RUNNING, BUT DON'T WORRY, IT IS MOSTLY ABOUT THE SYMBOLIC ASPECTS)

The years 2015 and 2016 were, to put it mildly, an uncomfortable and challenging time for me. There was plenty to be grateful for. I had a new partner and was in a happy, loving relationship, as indeed my ex would soon be. I had found a new manager. I was living a little more healthily, with minimal recourse to neat gin at lunchtime. All the same, after the professional and personal upheavals my own behaviour had put me through, the blows I'd taken and those I had inflicted on others, the task of rebooting my life felt too big and difficult to face up to. It was as if I'd had fifty sandcastles after a day's beach labour, seen an older kid trample them in the kind of destructive mania that sandcastles do bring out in certain children, and heard a parent – on the back foot – say, 'Well, why not build some even *better* ones?'

Part of the problem – as I've said – had been the repeated rituals, the stubborn performance of normality to disguise internal chaos. My new partner Lianne, now popularly known as Coop, encouraged me – from an early stage – to try to do more of the things that would make me happy rather than merely the things I felt I ought to be doing. Some of those things were no more complicated than going out for dinner or drinks and feeling like a human being – a likeable one, even – again. Some of them, though, had to do with reawakening parts of my brain that were buried under the clutter of the past few years; going back to basics. And some of the most basic compulsions in my brain are towards marathon projects: both figuratively and literally.

I had always wanted to run a marathon. Watching the 1988 Olympics as a child, I was mesmerised by the sight of the runners staggering into the stadium after a completely impossible-sounding *twenty-six miles*. It's the distance from Bristol to Bath and back, and, as far as I knew, you needed a car even to do it in one direction (as well as to carry back all the antiques which you went to Bath to buy in the first place). The idea of humans being able to run this distance, and not just run it but do it competitively – racing each other as if they were just in the school playground – was mind-boggling. And then the theatre of it: the final lap in the stadium itself, the cheering of 80,000 people as if they had all come there specifically to see *you* complete your mission. I watched every long-distance race that came on, marvelling at the ambition of it.

If you've been paying attention to my hubristic tenden-
cies and the misled daydreams which littered my early
years, you'll almost certainly be expecting me to say that
I fancied myself to be a future gold medallist and to end
up at least as famous as the men they made *Chariots of Fire*
about, but for once my thoughts had a sense of perspective.
I never imagined that it would be within my capabilities to
run a marathon one day. It didn't even really strike me that
long-distance running was a hobby one might develop as
an adult; I think I assumed that marathon runners were a
different species, specially bred in labs (which, unfortunately, was not so far from the truth about international
athletics in that era). That assumption was understandable,
because running was not something we did at school –
except when the rugby pitch was frozen and the teachers
had to devise the second-best means of torture available.
And it was nowhere near as popular as a recreational activity as it is now. If you saw someone running in our part of
Bristol in the early nineties, they were very likely in some
sort of trouble.

But the glamour of the marathon never really went
away and in my early thirties, when I began to try running, the idea swam into my head that perhaps I could
set the distance as an achievable target. By now, in the
early 2010s, running was a hobby that half the world had
adopted, and every April the London Marathon would
splash images of long-distance runners across the TV for
an entire Sunday morning. These people were no longer

all elite athletes, either: some of them were eighty-year-old women, people who'd recovered from deadly diseases, people who for reasons of their own had dressed as Mickey Mouse and were now sweating like meat in a butcher's window and cursing their existence as they crossed Tower Bridge. There was no mistaking the fact that it was, at least technically, within my grasp to accomplish what these emotional, medal-wearing people had.

The thought nagged at me every year between the ages of thirty and thirty-five; it became what would be called a bucket-list item. Throughout that period, though, I'd been holding myself back so instinctively and with such a vice-like grip that I wouldn't allow myself to believe *any* achievement was realisable. In that frame of mind, the idea of a 'bucket list' becomes ridiculous. When you have ceased to see the value in your being alive at all as I very nearly had, when you've lost faith in the idea that any of your actions can have positive consequences, hang-gliding or seeing Machu Picchu sink very quickly to the bottom of a list dominated by items like 'try to get to the end of the day without harming yourself in some manner' and 'avoid being in tears when you show up to collect your children from the school gates'.

But now that I was in a different setting mentally and physically, I found energy in a tank that had been empty a long while, and started running longer and longer distances. The day-to-day effect on my mental health was striking. A lot of people enjoy running, or walking, because they say it helps them collect their thoughts. For me, it was almost the opposite. My thoughts, as I've mentioned, are far too present all the time. I'm like one of these middle-aged men who are a bit *too* into their collections; I've got boxes of the things in my spare room and new thoughts are delivered in quantities that make my neighbours raise their eyebrows. This is not to claim that my thoughts are any more interesting, more creative, even more numerous than anyone else's. It's just that I have a hard time keeping them under control. With running, I found the release I'd needed for years.

When absorbed in long, hard runs I had no room for reflection other than, 'Ow, ow, ow' or, 'This is very long, isn't it?' Over long stretches of road or by the river I was unable to dwell on the mental litter I would normally be wading through. And when I got home, I found that the litter had magically disappeared, as if tidied up by the Rubbish Fairy or some other mythical environmental officer sarcastically conjured by one's mother. Running was giving me perspective; sometimes things are easier to see if you are not right in the middle of them. I became increasingly confident that I could handle long distances and more alive with the feeling of freedom. I began to tell myself that, before 2020, I would sign up to run a marathon.

Meanwhile, my team and I were hatching plans for a different kind of endurance mission: one of my twenty-four-hour shows. These shows had always been the opposite of the terrible driving-motorbikes-into-brick-walls TV series; they were things for which there was little professional argument but which made me feel fulfilled, even in the act of planning. And although these notions, of running and performing long-distance, ended up being deferred by the next twist in my career path, I did indeed end up pursuing them within a few months of one another and life on the other side of them would be – subtly, but importantly – different.

I'm not suggesting that either endeavour – running twenty-six miles or subjecting an audience to a full day of sleep deprivation – was what turned things around for me. What turned things around was learning a series of lessons about myself and what I needed in life, and finding the courage to seek out those things. And, as well as courage, patience.

The most obvious lesson to be drawn from anything that goes on for absolutely ages and makes you wait for the rewards is that a lot of life is about steady, incremental progress. Not rushing, not the scramble for minute-by-minute prizes which seems so seductive. This is yet another one of those truisms that I am forcing down your throat not because you don't know it, but because you might know it so well that you are ignoring it. The importance of the principle 'it's a marathon, not a sprint' is obvious when applied to an *actual* marathon, because if you sprinted for that long you would, unless you were Sir Mo Farah, likely die. Somebody like me, though, tends to sprint far too much.

If a day goes by without some major step forwards, if you have a week or period of weeks which brings discouragement or stasis, you start to panic that everyone is overtaking you and that you're losing ground. Once again, our constant state of connectedness tends to make things worse; the websites that we read as scoreboards, the obsessive tendency to see what others are up to and measure ourselves harshly against. And it's a bigger problem than just Facebook-anxiety: the relentless tempo of life in a digital climate.

The majority of us spend our days being paintballed with information, offers, images, background noise of all kinds. We can watch pretty much anything that's ever been made a few moments after it occurs to us to find it. Amazon Prime dispatches orders so quickly that they pretty much arrive before you've finished putting your credit card details in. We have become conditioned to think life is a race to accumulate both material things and achievements: a sort of endless *Supermarket Sweep*, to venture a reference that will divide this book's audience very cleanly into different age brackets.

Human life was never really meant to be like that, and hasn't become so just because we are now all supercharged, highly caffeinated creatures with unthinkably powerful computers in our pockets and handbags.

When you are running a marathon, there are some phases where things are not going particularly well, when your muscles start to go into revolt as they realise the full extent of what you've taken on and begin to enquire, 'What the fuck are we doing this for?' Your mental fortitude starts to waver as you are overtaken by someone dressed as Scooby-Doo and everyone cheers. For me, in Berlin – running what is to date my one, and probably only, marathon – this happened at about mile sixteen: quite a way in but, unfortunately, still a handsome ten miles from the point where I knew I never needed to run again in my life. Despite all the training, and despite what had been quite a promising first half, I felt extremely uncomfortable. Alongside the expected pains in my knees and back and soul, there was a tightness in my chest which I didn't like at all. I was forced to slow to the pace at which a newly retired couple make their way through a garden centre. My target finishing time became fantasy, very quickly; I had to face up to the fact that I was hardly even really running anymore. I was just surviving, one mile at a time.

An endurance comedy show has troughs of the same kind. Sometimes, no matter how impressive your guests at a given time, you are simply sapped of inspiration. Sometimes up to two-thirds of your audience is asleep and that does have a slightly draining effect upon your momentum, even if you fully understand and support their reasons. (It should be said, there are some hardcore people who never miss a minute of even a twenty-four-hour show; I worry for – but also depend upon – them and their ilk.) At those moments you have to resign yourself to a policy similar to the one that gets you through the seventeenth mile of a marathon: just keep going.

When I felt I had broken the back of the Berlin Marathon, knew in my guts I would finish it – somewhere between miles twenty and twenty-one – it wasn't because things had necessarily got easier or less painful, but because I had hung in there for long enough that I no longer feared the pain. In a marathon comedy show, I always know that things will be all right in the end, that the audience will be cheering and tearful or at the very least successfully persuaded by some form of Stockholm syndrome that they're happy. I've learned to accept the rhythms of these shows – including the bad bits. Sometimes in life you have to accept the bad bits, too – or, at least, understand that they aren't permanent. Some miles, some hours, are going to be slower and tougher than others. If you understand that in advance, it is much easier to ride them out.

Another useful lesson from the running type of marathon is the extremely literal demonstration of the truth that someone will always be ahead of you and someone always behind. The spectrum of ability in any running race open to the public – whether a half-marathon or a 10k – is one of the widest you will ever see at a supposed sporting event and the overall effect is really inspiring. To accommodate the large numbers of participants at big events (40,000 ran the London Marathon in 2019), the elite runners are sent off first – even though I think it would be much more fun to make them start at the back and send all the fancy-dress runners flying like skittles.

There's also something really liberating about this. You will never be as good at running as these people and you never *should* be; they've devoted their lives to it. On the other hand, there will also be somebody trailing about an hour behind you who put loads of work into getting ready for this race, but is so ill-suited to running that they will still be on the course when the roads reopen and a truck is sent around to pick up the stragglers. This is a real thing that happens and I imagine it doesn't feel that great; but even the people scooped up by that truck have themselves outperformed the thousands of people, like 2010 Mark Watson, who imagined signing up for the marathon and then thought, No, it's beyond me. Even getting to the start line of a race – again, with apologies for sounding a bit like Joe Wicks or some other exercise evangelist – is a sort of victory. Everyone in the race has won it together.

A lot of what we do is only meaningful because we're all doing it as a group. If you announced to someone that you had run twenty-six miles earlier that day, on your own and without previously informing anybody, your achievement would leave them fairly cold, especially when you tried to hit them up for twenty quid to go to a charity dedicated to rescuing birds or something. Twenty-six miles is an arbitrary figure, as we've said; it may be faithful to the original distance run by that poor man in ancient Greece, but if we were truly concerned with replicating his performance we would all have to drop dead after the run. What makes it worthwhile to run twenty-six miles and 385 yards – and let me tell you, those 385 yards aren't precisely what you're in the mood for by mile twenty-six – is that we *all* get together and do it. We train for months, we put on the inadvisable animal costume or the horrible but necessary little plasters that prevent nipple-chafing and, if we're not running ourselves, we stand by the road shouting encouragement or giving out jelly babies – thank you, by the way, you are heroes – or welling up at the TV because someone has staggered over the finish line in memory of their uncle. The marathon is a monument to the human ability to take something with no intrinsic value, and make it into an exercise in togetherness, in solidarity.

It's the same with the twenty-four-hour shows. There's no point in putting them on unless they build community with people who are also into the idea of doing a long, idiotic thing. Indeed, I've read about various people who have done their own marathon shows – I'm not going to use the phrase 'stolen the idea', because I don't own the copyright on the idea of 'a day', but . . . well, let's compromise with 'somewhat stolen the idea'. They found it was a lot less fun than they imagined, because their approach was just to rattle on, doing the same routines over and over again in a long cycle while the audience came and went. And if you aren't connecting emotionally with an audience, then they're not really an audience at all. What develops in my twenty-four-hour shows is, essentially, a long, hallucinatory party; performers and audience members unite in strange tasks; in fact people from the crowd become indistinguishable *from* performers.

What I've learned from long-distance running and long-distance comedy performing is that we are all better and stronger when we attempt things together. Variations on 'better together' have been hijacked by so many political causes and plastered across so many memes that we're sick of hearing the words in conjunction, but at their heart is something powerful and worth hanging on to. If life seems to you like the unwinnable battle that it was for me only a few years ago, it's because approaching things as a battle is unsustainable; it exhausts the spirit. Life might not be a game you win or lose, but it *is* something to be approached in a team. Your teammates are out there, if you can find them, or if you can let them find you.

7

DO SOMETHING YOU'VE NEVER DONE

None of the 'deaths' recorded so far in this book have involved much physical danger, really. But as lightning rips through the sky above me and the sound of sobbing fills my ears from both sides of the ditch I'm lying in, I taste what it's like to fear for my life in earnest and to be haunted by the truth that you don't know what you've got till it's gone.

The thunder splits our ears again. Each crack triggers a panicky wave of adrenaline and I begin to shake uncontrollably; I've been doing that on and off for four hours now. This is the fourth or fifth consecutive night like this and we can't tell how far through it we might be. We just know it is almost certainly going to get worse before it gets better. And it feels to me – as my worst nightmares play out in the heavens above – that there is no limit to exactly how bad 'worse' might turn out to be.

Are we GIs in Vietnam or doomed troops at the Somme? Is this the moment I spring the third-act plot twist that I am actually a time-traveller or have had multiple parallel existences? No, don't worry. It's just another reality show. But this time the reality is a brutal one. This time we are not just doing it for the cameras; we are doing it to survive.

In this contrived, but still very frightening situation, everyone else on the island is my teammate and only by trusting that idea can any of us survive. But that isn't the way we're encouraged to think, or to live. In fact, when you imagine the reality show I'm referring to, you are probably envisaging a competitive format, a last-man-or-woman-standing situation, such as insect-torturing favourite *I'm a Celebrity, Get Me Out of Here*. That's how most of these things work. It's what we're all conditioned to expect, after all: winners and losers.

If you aren't familiar with *Celebrity Island with Bear Grylls*, you're in the same camp as plenty of other people: probably including Bear Grylls himself, because he's only present for a couple of hours on the first day of the twenty-eight-day ordeal and a couple of hours on the last. Nonetheless, by the patchy standards of my broadcasting career it is something of a big deal. Grylls – whom you definitely *will* have heard of – is an internationally acclaimed survivalist. That means his job is quite literally not to die every day and, by that metric, you would have to say he is one of the most accomplished professionals the world has seen. His record is 100 per cent.

In case it sounds like 'surviving' is a fairly limited brief, it should be noted that Grylls places himself in considerably more perilous situations than most. He treks through the world's most hostile environments and fends for himself in places no human would ordinarily be able to live. I mean, it's almost as if the guy *wants* it to be difficult to survive.

The premise of the show is that ten personalities are sent to a seaside destination quite a lot lower down the pecking order than even Skegness; an uninhabited speck of land some way off the coast of Panama, largely peopled by vicious insects, spiky plants that cut you if you so much as lean against them, dense forest that you have to hack through with a machete, mangroves that you sink waist-deep into, and so on. We weren't given any food or water, and we had, of course, no contact with anyone back home (I could send Coop a weekly video message, but didn't know if they ever arrived, and could not hear back). It was, basically, a case of *I'm Not Quite Enough of a Celebrity to Be on* I'm a Celebrity, *Leave Me Here to Perish*. We could, of course, choose to leave at any time – by using the emergency radio to contact the mainland – but we were strongly discouraged from doing that. Some of our money would be deducted if we did and, of course, we would have the ongoing shame of having shirked the challenge.

I am not, in any sense, ready for this onslaught. We've been given a brief survival training course – and I can't emphasise the brevity of it enough. I'm the sort of person who needs to watch a YouTube how-to video before I attempt to open a bottle of shampoo; it was never likely that after an hour of watching the world's most accomplished outdoorsmen talking about things like 'A-frames' (which are structures you make out of logs in order to build outdoor shelters) and demonstrating different types of knot, I would be ready to go live with my own construction business. Even for the competitors far higher up the capability ladder than I was, the task of building a shelter in this desolate place would have been a challenge had the conditions been dry, but it is proving farcically difficult in weather as wet as this.

All the wood we try to use is too damp; our equipment keeps getting blown a hundred yards up the beach; our clothes are all soaking and our spare outfits got caught by the wind and blown into trees or into the ocean; most of our head-torches – one of the few luxuries in our island kit – don't work at all or break instantly due to the weather. And we have no drinking water except what we can lick from foliage as it pours out of the sky, because we haven't developed a decent system for catching water.

We have no food for a period that will end up lasting eight days. We haven't been able to get a fire going, because have I mentioned the damp? Which means no warmth, of course, but also no ability to prepare food and water without poisoning ourselves, even if we had caught any water. These are not ideal circumstances for ten near-strangers to attempt to stage an episode of *Grand Designs*.

We have built only the most basic of structures to keep off the torrential rain and we find ourselves clumped in little groups, in the darkness, the weather roaring at our defences again, the night pitch-black. Pitch-black, that is, except for the lightning, which illuminates the sky – and I'm not exaggerating – about once every twenty seconds for more than a twelve-hour stretch.

This isn't much fun for anyone, of course. One of our party, Lucy – a reality show star and successful entrepreneur – has apparent hypothermia and is being examined with alarm by our doctor; someone else is throwing up. The woman closest to me in the tent, an Olympian and physically powerful veteran of a million media appearances, keeps repeating, 'This isn't right. This isn't right.' Someone else is crying. At one point Ryan Thomas from *Coronation Street* seizes the radio – which we're only meant to use for emergencies – and asks if those at base camp could maybe send some sort of extra tarpaulin or temporary shelter, pointing out that the conditions are quite a lot more severe than we were led to expect, or than the producers themselves expected.

Understandably, the people at base camp, safe in their beds fifty miles away, are reluctant to do anything of the sort; the whole premise of the show is to see how close to our limits we can be pushed and, in fact, when the series does appear on the small screen, that exact phrase will be used in the trailer. One of our distant overlords tries to console us by using the expression, 'Try to hunker down until the morning,' which does very little, it's fair to say, to raise the collective mood.

'WE'RE FUCKIN' DYIN' HERE!' roars Ryan into the radio, which has – appropriately – gone dead itself.

It occurs to me – in desperate straits at three in the morning on the other side of the world from everything I love – that two things can be true simultaneously. On the one hand, we are not exactly victims here; we offered ourselves up quite voluntarily. We are not refugees or political prisoners or hostages; we are people getting paid and ultimately praised – maybe – for doing something inconvenient. Yet, all the same, this is as close to genuine helplessness, with all the terror that engenders, as any of us have been since we were babies. We are all aware that if something goes seriously wrong, we *could* be in genuine danger; all available help is a long boat ride away and, anyway, that boat can only arrive if the sea is safe, and it doesn't look like it ever will be. We are at least a week from the earliest point at which any of us could conceivably leave the show without being humiliated.

But I have an extra problem which nobody here knows about yet: a lifelong, animal-like, phobia of electrical storms. This is the stuff of my most pathological terrors. Every time the sky lights up, every time thunder goes off like a bomb, I genuinely think I am about to die.

There are twenty-four days to go.

★

It is, to say the least, the sort of thing you'd want to prepare pretty rigorously for. You'd want to put on some weight to compensate for what you're going to lose (we got an email from the producers to warn us that the body, after just a week in these conditions, starts to go into what is called 'starvation mode'; the same email cheerily remarked that 'death normally occurs between thirty and fifty days', which, given that the island trip was scheduled to go on for twenty-eight days, didn't feel like a *huge* amount of leeway). You might have some survival training, learn how to – say – tie a knot, which was something I'd never picked up in the Boy Scouts, largely because I had never been in the Boy Scouts. Of course not. I didn't want to camp in the cold or whittle tools with a knife; I wasn't living in the 1950s.

Now it seemed that those would have been pretty useful skills to have after all and that some extra pounds around the waist would have been quite welcome but, unlike the other nine participants, I hadn't been given time to make these preparations. I was only recruited a fortnight before we went into the wilderness. I'd been on a standby list, which involved being told that I *might* be going on a life-altering voyage but on the other hand I probably wasn't and, as a result, I spent an awkward morning at a travel clinic where I received three or four injections and then, when the doctor asked where I was off to, said, 'Well, probably nowhere, actually.'

But then the call came. Someone from the original line-up had dropped out after the pretty demanding medical that you had to take to demonstrate that you're a suitable person to be wrecked for the entertainment of Channel 4 viewers. In the way of TV people – who are the slowest in the world to respond to anything you send to them but simultaneously the most demanding of quick replies themselves – they needed to know that day.

I paced up and down for the best part of that day, 20 April 2017 (Hitler's birthday, although I'm not suggesting that had much bearing on my decision). The arguments against undertaking the show were numerous. I knew that it would not merely take me outside my comfort zone but deposit me in a place that was the polar opposite of that comfort zone and then send me an email that read, 'This is to notify you that your comfort zone has been destroyed and you must seek alternative accommodation going forward.' I knew there was the prospect of physical and psychological peril, although I couldn't have imagined at the time how much of either there would be. I would have no contact with any loved ones or friends for a month and I would miss an almost incalculable amount of sport. In fact, almost all of me did *not* want to go on to the island.

But the possible benefits were clear enough, as well. It wasn't merely that I had to make a living (there are, after all, easier ways to do that) or wanted to be on TV again (there are easier ways to do *that*, too; it would probably be less stressful to run naked into Buckingham Palace, and that would almost certainly do the trick). It was that I wanted to see whether the progress I'd tentatively made

– as described in the intermission earlier – was really worth anything. Whether all these ups and downs had truly led me to a place of greater self-respect and strength. When I spoke to a previous participant, my friend Josie, she said that the island was a valuable experience 'if you needed a, sort of, break from your life'. Stripped of all the baggage of normality, she implied, it would be a chance to confront who I really was and think about what further progress I wanted to make when I got home. All this sounded pretty much exactly what I needed, even if getting myself marooned on an island with near-strangers was a fairly circuitous way of going about it. 'My one was only two weeks long,' Josie added. 'I don't think I would have wanted to do it for a month.' I pretended to myself that I hadn't heard that part.

On my phone there was an image of a lonely figure gazing down from a frightening height, maybe about to hang-glide or bungee-jump or one of these other things people do if, mysteriously, their lives don't already contain enough terror. It said: 'IF YOU WANT SOMETHING YOU'VE NEVER HAD, YOU HAVE TO DO SOME-THING YOU'VE NEVER DONE.' I had spied this on the internet on the first day of 2017 and kept it as my screensaver for months, a reminder to have courage, to dare to aspire to a better life than the one I'd been mired in for quite some time. I stared at this little graphic. There was no point in subscribing to ideas like that in theory only, I thought, in having inspirational mantras popping up every time your phone locked, if you didn't attempt to live by them.

This was a clear case of two paths stretching out in front of me. One would take me into an unknown that could give me new confidence and belief and the other would end up with me watching someone else on the TV series when it aired and thinking, I wish I'd had the balls to do that. And so, even though almost everything to do with the *Celebrity Island* prospect filled me with dread, I knew I would not be able to live with the remorse of turning it down. It was a classic case of 'damned if you don't, struck by lightning if you do'.

I rang the producer. 'All right,' I said, 'I'm in.'

'Really?' said the producer, his voice rising in incredulity. It wasn't the most encouraging tone he could have adopted. But he was well within his rights.

You might have come across the statistic that there are 200 million insects for every human on the planet (perhaps in the Natural History Museum, or hissed at you by someone who wanted to ensure that you never sleep again) and struggled to believe it: how *can* there be that many, where would they all *live*? On this island just off Panama, it turns out: just waiting to introduce themselves.

When the sun went down – giving a brief respite from the fierce and muggy heat – we would hear the sound of the mosquitoes getting themselves ready for their evening out: a rising, purposeful hum like an orchestra tuning up. And the mosquitoes were only the tip of a writhing, nipping, blood-sucking iceberg. There were sandflies; horseflies; in fact, you could attach 'flies' to pretty much any other word and they would turn out to be there. There was no way of repelling these tiny predators and all of us were used as gastropubs by the bastards. In a way, the twenty-four-seven itching, the compulsion to tear my skin off, was symbolic of the minute-to-minute misery of living in this place. (If I'm dead and you're making a film of my life from this memoir, this would be an obvious visual motif to work with. Up to you, though. Good luck with the project.)

There was also the body's descent into starvation mode to contend with. I lost three stone, which might sound enviable to some, but I can promise you was not under those circumstances. Sleep deprivation arose as a consequence of all the above. All in all, I don't think any member of the group would have given it more than three stars on TripAdvisor.

But, as I mentioned with great subtlety at the start of this chapter, for me the most difficult element of all was more basic – the weather. I told the producers, when I signed up, that I was pretty jumpy around lightning. This was something of an understatement which I usually made because phobias aren't easy for others to empathise with. They try to use logic against what is an illogical terror, quoting statistics about how few people are struck by lightning every year or trying to comfort me with empty talk about how 'you're fine if you're not the tallest thing around'. This would only make me feel better if I was wandering into a storm with Richard Osman, which I rarely am. Or, they treat the phobia as a humorous quirk, because it doesn't square with their own experience of storms being a bit of a laugh ('Oh, I love a good storm, me. Let's go and run around in it! Here's a golf club to wave about and you can borrow my metal suit!'). The fact is that, most of the time, the fear has comparatively little to do with my actual chances of being hit by a massive bolt of electricity.

But my current location was the exception that proved the rule. I had underplayed my lightning-fear level while the show's production team had underplayed how many encounters with it there might be. They had said that we were going to the island 'on the cusp of the rainy season', but it was clear pretty quickly that this was a bit like saying Donald Trump had some policies that were on the cusp of being right-wing, or that a mouse is on the cusp of being small and squeaky.

The first week on the island was like a seven-day festival of extreme weather, without the consolation of a surprise appearance by Kylie and with even less in the way of adequate toilet provision. They were the most frightening nights of my life and I don't think that record will be broken until I have to face the most frightening thing of all – whatever awaits us at the end. Or I get locked in a ghost train, I guess: whichever comes first.

Since everyone else was also being dragged through the mill, I didn't feel like I could claim any extra sympathy for the fact I was not just miserable but virtually insensible with fear. I didn't even think I could tell them. The only way we were going to get through this was by means of a collective show of strength. We barely knew each other; I wasn't going to be the one who showed weakness. I was sick of always being the person who, when you tuned in to the show, you immediately said, 'Well, *he's* obviously toast.' The story I'd written in my head was that I was going to achieve something beyond what I had been capable of, and come back triumphant. I couldn't be whimpering my way through all this lightning and clinging on to people for protection.

What would Bear Grylls do? Well, he would climb out of this bunker, yell instructions at the sky until the storm stopped, then rip a couple of trees out of the ground and weave them into a reasonably priced budget hotel. I probably couldn't do that. But I could do my bit.

However, after a succession of what I now refer to as the Bad Nights, I couldn't really, anymore. I wasn't so much contributing as surviving. I tried to hide my head under various garments so the heart-attack-inducing pulses of bright light were at least a bit fuzzier. I made a lot of shaky-voiced jokes to cover the sound of the thunder. I repeatedly asked everyone else how they were doing, to distract from my own distress and tried to keep myself busy doing whatever little jobs I could do for the camp while maintaining no more than a semi-upright position – a peculiarity of my instinctive reaction to lightning is to sort of double over and hunch like someone with stomach problems, as if knocking six inches off my height might make the bolt seek out Osman instead. It was draining, both mentally and physically, to be clinging on like this, and eventually I didn't feel I could keep quiet anymore.

I told the group about the phobia, that I didn't know how much longer I was going to be able to withstand this International Storm Jubilee. About the idea that, even though we were all far beyond the end of our respective tethers, I had drifted so far away from mine that I wasn't sure I could make out with the naked eye where the tether was. And that I was going to have to ask to go home – confront failure – unless somehow they could find a place for me in the group as the virtual passenger, the liability, that I was. (I didn't use all of these phrases in full, but this was how pathetic I sounded in my own ears, and it *was* pretty much the shape of things.) It was the equivalent of the wounded soldier muttering, 'Go on without me, I'll only slow you down,' in a Sunday-afternoon war movie you might watch because you can't be bothered going to the pub. Except I wasn't oozing blood from a hole in my chest, which at least would seem like a legitimate excuse for bailing out of a Channel 4 series. I was just psychologically beaten down and I'd overestimated my ability to deal with that. I was the same low-status journeyman I'd always been and I wanted to go somewhere comfortable indoors and pull the duvet over my head.

What happened next taught me the beginnings of another important lesson. The response of the group was highly supportive – memorably so, considering they too had lost most of their clothes, minds and will to live. The actor from *Breaking Bad*, R. J. Mitte, offered the use of his special, thick ski jacket to huddle in, because the lightning would be all but invisible from under there (I became very attached to it and kept it after he left the show and have, in fact, still got it; at this stage, it seems safe to assume he's bought a new one).

One of the stoic camera operators attempted to take my mind off things during the most ferocious periods of the storm by telling anecdotes about her previous assignment. Unfortunately, her work had involved shooting a documentary about some sort of death squad connected to the drug cartels in Mexico. Instead of the sky falling apart I was now listening to someone murmuring things like, 'And the walls were covered – absolutely covered – in blood,' which was not much more relaxing than the storm itself. All the same, I felt accepted; it came to seem less likely that I would have to leave.

More than that, my confession paved the way for everyone else to start talking in more detail about the things that were driving *them* mad, too, and I heard things that I felt I could help with a little bit. By exposing my weakness to the group I'd added to our collective sense that there was strength in numbers; that this was something we could only do together. We started to make better decisions – to get a fire going and establish rotas for tasks and construct some sort of camp – in that spirit of collectivity. We had all come to understand that the survival of each one of us depended on each other one of us. This *was* something Bear Grylls had said, in his brief remarks before dumping us in this place – he isn't known as an expert for nothing – and within it lies a truth which applies to more than this very specific, and wet, environment. We are nothing without each other.

By the end of the week, we did have a fire going – a tiny, fragile flame, the result of many hours spent trying to get friction out of soggy planks and improvising kindling out of moss – and we now had to do whatever it took to keep it alive, because it was going to keep *us* alive, allowing us to feed, warm and hydrate ourselves. (You need to boil and filter water pretty thoroughly when it's come out of a swamp; we fashioned a system for doing this which involved cutting a plastic bottle in half and lining it with a pair of thick, khaki shorts to absorb a lot of the filthy sediment. They were, unfortunately, my shorts; I can't say I've had a lot of wear out of them since.)

The only way to protect the fire from the tantrums of the elements was literally to put our bodies on the line: when enough people stood around the fire, holding anything we could muster over the flame itself, we were able to keep it shielded. We had to work in shifts, some people holding a feeble plastic sheet over the precious fire while others bailed water out of other things that might function as covers, and gathered up any leaves that were approaching dryness in the hope of topping up the fire's sustenance. Pretty soon it was obvious that we were overstretched; we all had to abandon the thought of sleep and get our hands dirty for the whole night.

What this meant for me was spending an entire night in the crosshairs of the storm, lightning flashing in my eyes. The exposure to lightning and the sense of being an absolute sitting duck was something that, literally two weeks earlier, I would have considered beyond what I could tolerate as a person. If you are, for example, arachnophobic, it was the equivalent of someone placing around 150 spiders down the back of your neck over the course of an evening; or if you suffer from oikophobia, the fear of household appliances, I suppose it's akin to someone sneaking up behind you with a series of increasingly large toasters, whispering, 'Toaster!' in your ear.

The storm was on top of us for at least an hour that night. I had long given up the tactic of trying to count the time between crack and flash and using it to calculate the distance, because I could never even get as far as 'one', and the resulting data – 'The storm is twenty-seven centimetres away' – was providing little comfort. But here I was, all the same, out in the elements and, although I could feel my fearful instincts clamouring to take charge of my body and immobilise me, they weren't succeeding. I had passed through some sort of barrier.

It wasn't really that the previous storms had inured me, or I'd built up some resistance to the fear: the phobia was too deep for that. What I had learned was that if I had good people around me and if I allowed myself to rely on them, if I trusted to the fact I had something to offer them in return, I didn't have to undergo all the mental labour of fear on my own. It was shared by everyone. Just as a problem shared is a problem halved, a problem jointly tackled by ten people is only one-tenth of a problem for all of them.

On the sixth day, I came out fighting, ready to take this new courage-in-numbers and use it to face down the storm all over again. But on that sixth night the storm never came. The weather was calm; thunder rumbled away quietly from the direction of the mainland, without any real intimation that it was going to bother coming our way. I had survived the Bad Nights or, at least, the absolute worst ones. Or rather, *we* had survived them together. And this was a key finding, for me, because it wasn't as if these were people I'd known for years, necessarily had much in common with or, in some cases, would see again once the show was over.

Most of us subscribe to the idea that everything becomes more achievable with supportive friends, family or whoever it is we're lucky enough to be buoyed up by if we allow ourselves to be. This experience showed me that the truth is bigger than that. *All* of us are bound together during our brief residency on this habitable rock. I am only saying what most people I know believe, on some level – whether as a socialist, an empathy-practising citizen or simply a human who doesn't want to screw over other humans too much. I was never more aware of it, though, than when the size of society had been reduced to ten (plus camera crew), and each of us rose or fell through the wellbeing of the other nine. I couldn't help wondering if I could drag that understanding back with me to the world I more usually lived in. The one where there was a roof.

Sleep deprivation was another major factor to contend with on the island, even after I'd made some sort of peace with the thunderstorms. The thousands of insect bites, the difficulty of sleeping on palm leaves and in clothes with a very low tog count, the longing for friends and family – all of it inflicted a level of insomnia unlike anything I'd experienced. Most nights, I abandoned the idea of sleep altogether and paced endlessly up and down a stretch of beach about fifty metres long, hemmed in by rocks on both sides, listening to the sea lap at the shore.

About two o'clock one morning, with less than ten days until the finish, I was doing my usual rounds of this limited space when I found a bottle of whisky that had washed up along with the usual payload of junk. This happened every day and provided a terrible reminder of the reckless habits of mankind – so much plastic, so many things discarded after minimal use, some of the items left to drift hundreds of miles after, in many cases, having been shipped thousands of miles in the first place. This bottle was one of the first genuinely interesting items to fall into our hands – apart from the odd usable fishing net and flip-flops – and even this bottle was, naturally, pretty much empty. But not quite. It had been sealed and discarded with a tiny amount of whisky, a quarter of a shot, still inside. Even the smell of the neck was, after nineteen days of next to no food or drink at all, enough to get me tipsy. I wrenched off the top – using all of the next day's supply of energy – and drank the syrupy drop from the depths of the bottle. I raised the bottle in salutation to the moon.

I knew that across the continents, the UK would be waking up. It wasn't the middle of the night back home anymore, even if it was here. There was warmth and weight to that thought. The once-frightening grip of the night seemed brittle now, easily shaken off. That night, and over those that followed, I began to think in more depth about what I was going to take from this 'break from life' and how I'd apply it to what was waiting for me when I returned.

Of course, the vast majority of us are not – unless something has gone terribly wrong – spending time on an island with nothing but coconut shavings and a 98 per cent heavy precipitation forecast. Most of the time, we're at large in that real, roof-bearing world, and in this world the rules are set to make us forget we're a team. Under most systems of government, in most areas of the western-capitalist world, it's nearly impossible not to fall into the trap of thinking that life is a scramble to the top. But now, pacing up and down the beach every night, with nobody but this micro-society of people to measure myself against, I felt I'd understood something which had eluded me for so many of the difficult years: not only do you not *have to* do it on your own (as I'd come to realise), but you literally *can't*. Whatever your political position or opinions on how society should be ordered, you can't get away from the fact other people are here. From that point, it isn't much of a jump to understand that an alliance of all these people leaves us all richer than a limbs-flailing competition to grab an advantage here and there before we each die.

I knew that once I returned from this fever dream to living in a society with more than a dozen other people in it, it would be harder to hold on to this conviction. I would quickly be sucked back into the race. An hour after arriving at the basic hotel that was the first staging-post on the way to civilisation, I would already have transitioned from, 'What a miracle to hold my phone in my hands again, to have everyone I love at my fingertips once more' to, 'It's frustrating I'm not allowed to tweet this picture of myself with bites all over my face and a thousand-yard stare; people would be retweeting it left, right and centre.'

After a few weeks in a human zoo like London, back in the ego-wrestle of my career, I reflected, all the old instincts would very likely resurface. I wouldn't be able to see another comedian doing well without feeling that I myself had fallen short of some imagined target. It would be as if this island – with its very occasional flashes of beauty, the chalky moon rising over the dark ocean at night, the birds flying in long formation, the sigh of the sea – had never existed, and all the insights I had gained here would be just like the seeming revelations that arrive in dreams and can't be grasped again with the daylight. But I knew I would always be able to summon, in an instant, the memory; revert mentally to this place, where ego and status didn't matter, where all that counted for anything was the ability of one person to make life a little easier for the next person.

I had worked out something about how to live. In a very short time I would be on the other side of it and I would have completed the challenge they set for me, proved something about myself, at last. I would have won.

Then, only a week from what should have been the end of my time on the island, things went to hell quite suddenly. The long procession of sleepless nights had taken more of a toll on my wellbeing than I was aware of, or at least had been admitting to myself. I started to get some fairly pronounced chest pains. I don't want to descend into medical mumbo-jumbo, but a lot of doctors think chest pain can be bad news and very few of them see it as a positive indicator. My teammates (by now my friends) made me lie in the one raised bed we had – expertly built out of timber by a former Pussycat Doll. It was extremely uncomfortable, like lying on a bed if you removed the mattress, but by the standards of the camp it was a four-poster. Rather than sleep I descended into a series of unpleasant hallucinations and the pain continued. The camp's doctor, Sara, examined me and was concerned enough to send for the show's health and safety supervisor. Because this was now classed as a medical emergency and every second might count, the boat was there in not much more than three hours.

The supervisor, Aidy – like every member of Bear Grylls's team, a really lovely and kind person – asked me a series of questions which are now difficult to recall. This whole twenty-four-hour period only features in my memory as a blurry set of images, like an LSD montage in a BBC drama aimed at the younger end of the demographic and used by politicians to complain about the licence fee. I later saw that in his medical report he said that I was 'ranting and raving quite a bit', but it's hard to see how he was able to differentiate between this and my normal state of being. I managed to persuade him that, if he gave me another twenty-four hours, I would be fine; I'm not sure whether I believed that or was just hell-bent on getting to that imaginary finish line in which I'd invested so much significance. I was not fine, though, and the following day Aidy was back again, this time with a couple of sturdy boatmen in hi-vis jackets – roughly how you picture the last people you see before you die. He squatted down next to me; I was in a foetal position in the sand.

'I'm going to make the decision for you, mate,' he said. 'I'm taking you off.'

Numb, I said my goodbyes to the people who had got me through this. I was filmed radioing the base camp with my decision to leave, although it hadn't really been my decision and it was something of a formality as the boat was already here. I was helped into the boat and given a bottle of water, which I stared at for a little while, like a cow asked to write its name with a Sharpie. I was taken to the production hub, checked by medics, examined and interviewed for the cameras. They were the opposite of the interviews I'd been rehearsing in my head on those night walks. Those interviews had been all about how it felt to triumph in this trial by fire. I had phrases like, 'The real battle is against yourself, not against the island,' all ready to roll. Instead, the questions were about how it felt to be 'the fourth person to leave'. About whether it was disappointing 'not to have made it to the end'. The questions were about what it was like to be a failure.

The disappointment stayed with me for at least two weeks after I got home – nice as it was to be back, to have a phone, a toilet and access to jelly babies (which I had mysteriously come to crave while marooned off Panama and which I now spent much of the day either eating or thinking about). I'd been within eight tough days of ac-complishing something huge. Instead, I would go down as the plucky loser, the guy who wasn't quite up to it; I might as well be the 'Celebrity Storage Hunter' motorbike victim all over again. Maybe it was my fate after all to be *that guy*.

It wasn't until the others started to return that I came to see things differently. I spoke to two of my fellow former inmates, comedian Shazia Mirza and sprinter Iwan Thomas, not long after the plane brought them back. The final week had been horrendous, they said; the storms started all over again, there was even a tornado; one of them had literally prayed for their life on the penultimate night.

'But it must have felt amazing to have got through that?' I asked.

'Not really,' both of them said.

'You got out at the right time. You'd already proved yourself,' as Iwan Thomas put it. 'So had we. All we did was just suffer all over again.'

'But you must feel like you've changed in some way, found out something special about yourself?' I pressed. Again: not really, they both said. Both of them – unlike me – had always assumed they would definitely finish the full twenty-eight days, for a start. Getting to that goal hadn't represented some sort of miracle for either of them; it was just fulfilling their expectations. Whereas, when I looked at what I had managed to do, it was far more than had ever seemed possible, either when I was first asked to be on the show or when I was writhing in fear at the lightning and contemplating having to leave almost before people at home had finished sending their good-luck messages. I had won, by my own standards, even though I hadn't completed the show; Shazia and Iwan felt no sense of victory, even though they *had*, because the standards they set themselves were different.

The real lesson of the entire experience wasn't that I had battled the odds, or my fellow islanders, and 'won'. It was that I needed to abandon the whole idea of winning and losing, as I was used to thinking about it. I had to get back to that sense of life as a piece of music, something you are meant to dance to the rhythms of, immersing yourself in its tonal shifts and jolts and different tempos, rather than trying to blast your way through it.

When I first brought this idea up, I said that I had got it from Derren Brown, and it's true: he evoked it, beautiful-ly, in his live show *Miracle*. Paraphrasing Alan Watts, he said 'you forget that maybe life should be more like a piece of music and you're supposed to be dancing.'

When I heard these words in the theatre, not long after coming back from the island, they made me cry, although I pretended it was an allergic reaction, something I'd picked up during the time away (I was able to pass off almost any sort of behaviour, from excessive sneezing to sweating in the night to a sudden fondness for eighties power ballads, as 'something I'd picked up'). As I said earlier, I've never been a dancer at all and am suspicious of people who can do it, want to do it or can predict how the scores will go on *Strictly* (I wouldn't have a clue whether a dance had gone well or badly unless someone's trousers fell down and they headbutted one of the judges). But this was the point, perhaps.

Maybe the reason I didn't 'get' dancing was for similar reasons that I'd not 'got' life for long stretches of it. Because I was, as Brown diagnosed, always forging towards the goals, the endings, and not enjoying what was happening *now*. Because I was always trying to control things rather than submit to the glorious, out-of-your-hands abandon, the embrace of the universe's chaos, which you see when someone truly loses it on the dancefloor. Because I have always tried to win every game, rather than rip up the idea of winning and losing and just wade into the throng.

And it's significant that Derren Brown – one of my main go-tos for worldly wisdom – is himself, here, just summarising the findings of a wise person before *him*, who will probably have got it from his mum or from an old washerwoman he met in the Andes, and so on. Firstly, it's a nice thought that the knowledge that we should be dancing through life is built into all of us somewhere, even me, even people who have somehow never come across the Bee Gees song which quite literally frames it as an imperative. Also, when you think someone is possessed of some insight that you envy them for, the chances are they've just got the echo of a thought someone had before them.

When I began thinking about writing this book, some time ago now, I looked at the sum total of my career and had quite a strong feeling that I had unique things to say about failure, about mortification, the ways in which those apparent knockbacks can be repurposed as successes or stepping stones. Then I did a bit of research and found that an enormously popular book on this subject had been published even in the past year: *How to Fail*, by Elizabeth Day – by coincidence someone I met at university.

Does it diminish my efforts, to know that people have already said lots of what I have managed to say here? Yes, and it's bloody annoying that their books did so well and Elizabeth Day also has a successful podcast and, all in all, I might as well print this off and then consign it straight to the bottom of the ocean.

Sorry, the positivity slipped for a moment there. Let's try that again.

No, it doesn't mean that at all. It just illustrates that all of us are players together of a giant game that nobody can ever truly master and all of us chip in our tiny amount to the collective stack of hints and tips we've amassed. We are all, as a human race, like people wandering around Hampton Court maze, helpfully exchanging information like, 'It isn't this way, we've already tried this way!' or, if you're anything like me, just muttering, 'Why would I sign up to get lost for entertainment when I spend half of my life being lost or late for things anyway?' (See also: escape rooms.) The fact that I can be in the middle of planning a book about the beneficial or educational fallout of failure and find that someone has already written such a book, and is seemingly on every radio station worldwide to talk about it, only underlines what I'm talking about in the first place. *You can't even win at not winning.*

But you don't have to. Every life is a combination of little victories and defeats, and nobody but you gets to decide what the final score is. In fact, there *is* no final score. The only way you'll ever be able to take a proper account of the whole long, complicated, intricate, multi-character story is when you're about to die. And by then, of course, none of it's going to matter as much as you thought it did at the time.

We'll come back to that in a second, though. Before we leave me – your host, Mark Watson – let me take you to one more, all-too-recent, gig. Considering it's almost fifteen years since that first mortification on stage, surprisingly little has changed in some ways. You can die on stage in your ten thousandth show just as easily as in your first.

8

YOU'RE USELESS, MATE

There is a dickhead on stage. Again. He's saying stupid things. Nobody wants him to be there; he's making everyone uncomfortable. He's had too much to drink. There's no obvious way to stop him from embarrassing himself as he lurches from bad to worse. He should be old enough to know better than this, but some people never seem to learn.

Wait, though. This time, the idiot is *not* your comedian, Mark Watson. It's a guy in the audience. The trouble is, this gig is at a corporate function, and so the 'stage' isn't really a stage; it's just a floor with a mic placed in the middle, the dinner tables encroaching on the sides of what should be the playing space. In a sense, you could say this isn't even an audience, not in the traditional sense of 'a group of people who have either paid, or at least willingly assembled, to watch something'. They are a collection of delegates at a black-tie dinner, united only by the fact that they all work in the coffee wholesaling industry. The man making a nuisance of himself, for example, is a middle manager for a coffee company. This is a boom industry, of course, thanks to these maniacs who have a print in their kitchen with a clockface that says 'COFFEE O'CLOCK!' at every point from one to twelve, as if that sort of approach to life would lead to you being productive and sparky, rather than – after your eighth coffee – charging into a meadow, punching a bull and then jumping into the river.

This manager, to be fair to him, didn't expect to be listening to a comedian tonight; he expected to eat a functional meal of hunter's chicken and potatoes, network in the bar with other pawns of the caffeine fraternity and go home to have disappointing sex. But here, all the same, is the comedian, with the audacity to stand up and steal twenty minutes of his chat-time. He's put out that he has to pay attention, and so he doesn't.

He mutters a couple of things to his wife and colleagues; because he's so close to the non-stage, this is pretty distracting, but the comic is a naturally polite person, averse to confrontation, opposed to the aggressive tactics which many other entertainers deploy in these situations. (There is an oft-told story about an act who was so riled by chatty audience members that he leapt on to their table, simulated masturbation in front of them and yelled something to the effect of, 'Different things are considered rude.')

For the first few minutes of these disrespectful antics, mindful that I was being paid for this and part of that fee comprised danger money to compensate me for exposure to idiots, I soldiered on. In previous shows, I might well have continued soldiering on for my entire time on stage. But this is the late 2018 Mark Watson, a person who is less inclined than he was to allow others to shape his self-respect or his sense of success and failure. It's not quite the unstoppable force against the immovable object, but things *are* about to get interesting. It happens that, only weeks earlier – in the warm summer of 2018 – I have set a precedent for looking after myself a little better.

There is a dickhead in the front of the car. But, once more, it's not our hero. It's an ex-military man turned driving instructor – already a dubious career path, you might think – who has been tasked with teaching Watson to drive, from scratch, almost exclusively on dual carriageways, for the entertainment of all the people who watch E4 – my fingers typed the word 'all' there only after hovering for some time over the keys for the word 'both'.

I have never learned to drive – and with good reason. There are some people who should not be allowed behind the wheel of a car. Many of them nonetheless hold driving licences – you see them every day. Knowing your limitations is important and is not inconsistent with standing up for yourself; you aren't meant to be able to do *everything*. It's as Mother Teresa said: 'We cannot all do great things on this earth. Especially not me; it's much too bloody hot today.'

Among my limitations – motoring-wise – are the facts that I have pretty poor spatial awareness, make bad decisions under pressure and am usually drunk. You'll recall that my previous adventure with a vehicle led to a collision with a wall. A lot of people would have taken from that incident the insight that it was time to move away from the genre of 'TV shows where you are given a potentially life-ending machine to control'.

Yet I've signed up for the show, all the same, thinking that it would undeniably be a useful life skill to have, and that maybe I'll benefit from the constrained learning schedule; that it will spark me into applying some kind of effort that would normally be beyond me. Perhaps these intensive courses *do* work like that for some people, but not for someone like me. For a person of my temperament, trying to learn to drive a car under a harsh time limit makes no more sense than being given control of a 747 midway through its runway taxiing with the words, 'You'll get the hang of it as you go along.'

Is the instructor sympathetic to these anxieties as we steam along the dual carriageway at a speed a person shouldn't drive if they're not yet sure which pedal is which? Apparently not; on the contrary, he is urging me to apply even more gas. 'I want to see fifty, I want to see fifty!' he yells, excitably, and it crosses my mind: I too would like to see fifty, but I don't think we mean the same thing by it.

And, once more, however obliging I am, however professional and polite I've already tried to be and however grateful for the work, there is a sense here that if I've learned anything along the more metaphorical road of the last few years, it's that I need to put the brakes on pretty quickly. It's just, I would need to know which pedal does that.

'Life comes at you fast,' people were fond of saying online a couple of years back – normally with reference to someone who had been publicly proved wrong; for example, being photographed crunching on an apple only six months after tweeting, 'Apples are shit and if I ever eat one you can shoot me.' And sometimes, it's true, it does. But, to come back to the 'marathon, not a sprint' motif: one of the biggest challenges about life isn't necessarily that it flings a lot of dramatic stuff at you at once, but that it just keeps on going, keeps looking for ways to mess you up or, at least, it makes very little allowance for your vulnerability (to put it in a slightly less paranoid-sounding way).

When you emerge from one of life's tunnels into a patch of bright light, when you have taken on and beaten some of the things that were holding you back, it is easy to feel that everything is going to be different from now on. An awful lot of the messages we see around us encourage this way of thinking, this narrative: 'Things used to be wrong, now they're right!' 'I had all these things I needed to change – now I have, and I rule the world!' A large industry rests on selling you this very attractive idea and it works because we want to believe it. But even when things are good, they aren't going to be good *every single day*. And even when a wound is healed it can still ache from time to time.

I had a right to be proud of the distance that I had travelled, but you rarely travel in a straight line through life, even when things are going well. Sometimes there's a bit of reversing to do. The acceptance of that fact is important, even though it goes against your instincts and feels as wrong as reversing on an actual motorway. At least, I *assume* you can't do that. We didn't get anywhere near that bit of the course.

Corporate events, like this coffee convention which fell a few weeks after the driving show, are famously well-paid, but have a forbidding reputation. When people say, 'I'd rather die than stand up in front of people and do *that*,' the abstract, awful things they're imagining are mostly to be found in a bad corporate gig. (During lockdowns, a friend of mine – Joz Norris – tweeted about a terrible online gig he performed for a business, which concluded with the client interrupting his struggling act and commanding him to 'do something else'. My colleague responded by playing 'Happy Birthday' on the clarinet, hanging up, and then bursting into tears.)

If I've got slightly more of these war stories than some, it's probably – as ever – because of my combination of trusting nature, work ethic and masochism. My very first corporate booking was for a Cardiff firm's 'family fun' day. I was asked to do half an hour of stand-up and to keep it clean, because there would be kids present. Fair enough, I thought. It wasn't as if most of my act was particularly offensive to anyone, anyhow, and I wasn't scared of an indifferent audience if the prize on offer was the largest fee I'd ever commanded for a gig. What catch could there be? Well, there were quite a number, it turned out. Alarm bells began to ring as soon as I was shown to the perform-ance space, to give it a wildly over-generous name. It was less like a comedy venue and more like a soft-play area; the 'family fun' aspect of the occasion involved pre-school children romping all over the stage while their grim-faced parents sat and listened to whatever comedy I could make audible over the sound of their offspring.

A couple of the intruders were slightly older and of a mind to interact with me, which didn't entirely fit my plans but which I tried to see as a challenge that needed to be embraced. 'Do *you* know any jokes?' I asked, partly with humorous intent, but partly thinking that if this child-centric mayhem was the general vibe of the whole thing, I might as well go with it. One of the kids, who was probably about nine, took the microphone off me. I encouraged the crowd to clap and cheer him. At last, people were focused on the stage. I had adapted, I had improvised.

The kid told a racist gag, the sort of material you'd have heard in a working men's club in the seventies in the days when you could (extremely pronounced inverted commas here) 'say whatever you wanted without the PC brigade stepping in'. An icy silence fell over the room – except for the chuckling of a handful of misguided people, whose laughter was the loneliest sound in the world. In the same way you sometimes think you hear voices in the wind, I fancied I could hear the silence whispering to me, 'You're in a lot of trouble now, old mate, get the mic back off the kid and get the hell out of Cardiff.'

The day after the gig, my agent told me there'd been several complaints about 'my offensive material' and the Cardiff company was threatening not to pay me. I said the material in question had come from a kid who'd got involved in the show because the organisers had not thought to ask people to prevent their kids running on the stage. My agent backed me and invoiced for the full fee. Nothing happened. I became a little anxious because the fee amounted to more than a month's rent and my early experiences of London life had taught me that landlords were really keen on having rent on time; it was one of their favourite things, in fact. We kept asking. Another week passed – by now, I had sold our toaster on eBay – and the agent called again, sounding somewhat apologetic.

'There's good news and bad news,' he said. 'Bad news is, the entire company has gone out of business, by the look of it.'

'Right . . . and the good news?'

'That was more just a figure of speech,' he said.

Not all of my worst corporate experiences concluded with a company imploding; some of them ended with me merely fantasising about that happening. There are many charlatans in the comedy industry, of course, many murky corners of activity, but when you start working as a hired clown for different businesses you are brought into contact with a different realm of chancer-dom altogether.

I did an event for a magazine publisher and, while I was changing in the hotel, the editor of the magazine came in, said that she needed the room to do her hair and threw me out. I made a joke about it on stage and the next day they tried to withhold my fee. Another time, I flew home from Sydney to host an awards ceremony for a company whose line of work was the collection and removal of vinyl flooring. That's right, Sydney: so, a twenty-five-hour commute to avoid letting these people down. When I got there, straight from the flight and after a two-hour car journey, I found they'd not got me a dressing room and I had to bribe someone at reception to let me into a board-room, where I pulled my suit on in front of a less than full-length mirror.

The event went well, even though the company was so far down the food chain and the awards so non-prestigious that quite a lot of the winners hadn't even bothered to show up. Afterwards there were quite a lot of handshakes and selfies and a general atmosphere of satisfaction. On the Monday, I found out they were trying not to pay me because 'my shirt had been too creased'. Again, we won that argument, but I've still got the name of that unscrupulous CEO on my phone in case he ever tries to book me, or anyone I know, again. Not that I really need it on my phone; 'Andy Rogers' is burned into my brain. My blacklist isn't all that long, but it's rigorously maintained. (That wasn't his real name, of course.) You can see a pattern emerging: the shonkier the business, the tighter their profit margins, the more likely it is that they'll try to swindle you after the event.

That was not going to happen with these caffeine dignitaries; my manager had secured part of the fee as a deposit. All the same, this man was starting to get to me. His chair was angled away so that he didn't even have to watch me. It is pretty rude to do this when a performer is on stage doing their best to entertain you, the equivalent of inviting someone round for dinner and then making them eat it in a separate room. I reproached him mildly for this. He turned around to face me for what was the first time. 'You're useless,' he muttered.

'Sorry?'

'You're useless, mate,' he said again.

Even at this advanced stage of my career, this might ordinarily have been enough to make me think that the fault was mine; to lose confidence. But something in my head wasn't going to let that happen, this time.

As you'll already have gathered from previous chapters, there are plenty of unworthy characters in the TV game, too; the industry is infested with them like an old building overrun by Japanese knotweed. This isn't to be lazy and say that everyone in television is some sort of Hollywood caricature of a showbiz bad guy – gold teeth, a cigar and a swimming pool out the back, snapping, 'OK, you got ten seconds' as a nervous young assistant comes in with a pitch she's spent her life working up to. Of course, there *are* proper villains in the business, as we're reminded every now and again by the revelation that a once-great name has been 'cancelled' for sexual offences ('cancelled' in this context meaning 'encouraged to issue a statement of regret and stop making work for a very brief period, then return with a Netflix special after three months or so'). But a lot of the most depressing figures in TV don't become that way because of actual malignity. It's more that they're aware the time in which they can make money might be limited and is dependent on factors beyond their control. They're making the absolute best of what they've got. If that means they have to make the best out of what *you've* got, without regard for consequences, then they'll do it. If they have to throw you out of a hot-air balloon be-cause their salary rests on a show they've managed to get commissioned called *Minor Celebrities Fall Out of a Balloon*, they'll do it before you can complete the sentence, 'I'm pretty sure the contract said a *metaphorical* balloon.' If it's not you falling, it's them. We are, to use a term that's come back into fashion, all grifters. And grifting means you do what you've got to do.

This applies to people on both sides of the camera. As a performer or a maker of shows, you're pretty disposable, one of a long line of people with similar skills. This was the case with the driving show. The instructor had built up a specific persona on the show – motormouth, bit of a lad, an adrenaline guy. He was aware that the most comically inappropriate way he could deal with someone like me would be to push me to places that I wasn't comfortable going – a very busy roundabout, for example, or the slipstream of a lorry. He knew that if he didn't make me anxious, it wouldn't be as entertaining a TV show, the producers would be less inclined to keep him as one of the instructors in future series, and the good thing he'd got going would be in danger of slipping away from him. Even if he wasn't consciously putting all this together in his head, he was instinctively acting this way because he understood the grift.

Same, again, with the makers of the show. They were aware they were fortunate to be getting paid to make something, even if it *was* so bad that they would spend most of their time at parties saying, 'Er, no, nothing you'd have heard of.' They knew that if they didn't squeeze the wafer-thin concept for every drop of entertainment possible, the guy who commissioned it could very easily pull the plug, replacing it with a show where affordable celebrities went white-water rafting or learned to skateboard or make cheese and they would be out of the only steady job they had.

People act irresponsibly for all sorts of reasons that are out of your hands. The man at the corporate evening was trying to assert his status, consciously or otherwise. The man urging me to drive faster, regardless of the effect on my blood pressure, was trying to hold on to *his* position. You are always at the mercy of what life has done to other people.

But that doesn't mean you have to cave in. For most of my life I have been in the business of backing down to people who were louder, bossier, more insistent; just bolder. As I looked into the eyes of the man insulting me at my work, and as I sat terrified at a roundabout, I thought: No, this stops here. This is not going to be another death. I have learned to survive.

It's an ongoing and conscious effort to remind yourself of the things you've learned about how to live. Like everything else, good thoughts need to be practised. Just as you need to keep playing piano scales until they become second nature, or type out variations on the Spanish for 'I have not bought a hat today' (even when you're begging the Duolingo bird to let you stop or at least change the subject), you have to keep reminding yourself again and again of the progress you've made.

Nobody can or should tell you how to live your life; achievements and goals matter less than contentment; you are not constantly winning or losing, life is a subtler process than a game. If you have taken anything remotely useful from what I have said so far, it won't automatically sink into your brain and pop out helpfully again every time you need it. You will, instead, have to keep saying it to yourself, keep relearning it, over and over again. The mental muscles that keep you thinking the right way, treating yourself with kindness and respect, have to be exercised (yes, sorry to mention it again) like *actual* muscles.

Some people go so far as to write down rules, affirmations or mantras. They hang them up, read them out regularly. This is the sort of practice I would have poured scorn upon in my twenties, spent my thirties reluctantly accepting was probably not the worst idea and am planning to gracefully come round to in my forties, adopt in my fifties and start mocking all over again in my sixties, because by that age you can dismiss pretty much anything you want as 'a load of nonsense'.

I've never quite been the sort of person who takes easily to reading things out loud. During a writing course at which I was a tutor, my co-host Emma Jane Unsworth got everyone to write out a list of 'Desiderata' – a manifesto, a reminder of the things they wish they could say to themselves. Even though I found the exercise surprisingly moving, almost to the point it brought me to tears, and even though I went away thinking, I'm going to pin that up somewhere and consult it every time I need to, the resolution didn't last any longer than the flush of wine that brought it on.

What I have tended to do with pearls of wisdom that, ideally, needed to be put on a psychological shelf for me to polish and inspect is, instead, to bury them in a safe deep at the bottom of an ocean and not look at them until and unless life absolutely forced me to. As you'll know if you've ever cleared out your attic, once something's been in storage for a long time it's difficult to predict what sort of state it'll be in when you open it up. If you're not in regular contact with important feelings and emotions, they will find a way of getting in contact with *you*. And they probably won't choose a convenient time.

'You know how roundabouts work,' said my hyperkinetic instructor. He was telling rather than asking me. This was wishful thinking, to put it politely. What I knew about roundabouts was that they had multiple exits, required quick thinking, and regularly caused even experienced and capable drivers I knew to say things like, 'Shit, which lane am I meant to be in?' or, 'We're going to have to go round again' or, 'It's a shame you don't have a driver's licence because I think I might just get out of the car and walk into the traffic, here.' What I knew about this particular roundabout was that I felt enormously keen *not* to try to drive around it, in a throng of HGVs and other motorists afflicted by the permanently furious expressions of many of their kind.

I suppose it was technically true that I 'knew' the rudiments of roundabout etiquette because I'd had to pass the theory test before signing up. But as you'll be aware if you have taken that test yourself, it is possible to pass it with enormous gaps in your knowledge. The randomised nature of the questions means you can quite easily get over the required pass mark by sidestepping tricky stuff like roundabouts or parking and instead nailing a series of multiple-choice questions like: 'Someone asks you to open a packet of fireworks while you are driving and set one off in the car: do you (a) just go for it, (b) have a rest by the side of the road first, (c) refuse?' The fact I'd seen a diagram of the way cars are meant to address a roundabout absolutely did not mean that I was capable of performing that action myself, any more than having watched *Blue Planet* means that I can grow gills and start living under-water. Tempting as that idea was starting to seem.

'OK, here comes the gap,' said the instructor. Crouched behind me in the back seat was a cameraman, his lens a few inches from the back of my neck. Sweat glued my T-shirt to my back. My hands were greasy on the wheel (again, from sweat; if I'd been eating a pasty as we were driving along, I would deserve less sympathy). It was hot and stuffy in the car and I had begun to feel pretty unwell.

Across the dashboard sat the set of emergency dual controls with which the instructor could seize command from a trainee in the event that the driver in question completely loses his shit. My instructor – and I'm con-tinuing to describe him by that charitable name – had already pointed these out numerous times in an effort to convince me that, whatever happened, we would be safe from harm. My feeling was that 'harm' could take many forms. If we got close enough to an accident that he had to deploy these controls, that would be more than enough to mess with my brain.

Still, he now tapped the controls as if they were a set of magic wands and gave me a sidelong look. His feet were jiggling on the floor; he wanted action. I tried to spot the 'gap' that he was urging me towards. I could only see a steady stream of large vehicles driven by people who were on their way to appointments of one kind or another and probably did not want to be held up by involuntary participation in a reality TV show. My heart rate was about where you might expect an SAS operative's to be in the moments before being dropped into a war zone.

'Go, go, go, go, go!' yelled the instructor, as if he *was* fighting a war. I froze, my hands useless on the wheel. 'Oh, you've missed it, you've missed it!' he lamented. I plunged my foot down on the accelerator and tried to get into a gap that very definitely did not exist anymore. This was not a good strategic decision.

We went hurtling towards the back of a Mercedes. I had a sick-making wave of panic, the instructor slammed on the dual-control brakes, we went tumbling forwards in our seats and came to a stop inches from impact. I was shaking uncontrollably. My companion took control of the teacher's steering wheel, got us around the roundabout, and we drove back to the production base in silence.

After sitting around for a couple of hours with nobody to talk to, gradually trying to return my shredded nerves to some sort of order, I was told an exec was coming to see me. You always know they're worried that they've crossed a line with you, on a TV show, when an 'exec' appears. As far as I can tell, their general role is to move in when things are already underway, stand on the set with their phones out, eating Pret A Manger sandwiches, saying, 'Yep, all seems to be going great,' and then, when the show struggles to get ratings, say, 'I had my concerns all along.' They generally only need to get involved on set if something has gone really badly wrong or if the show's becoming successful and they need to be visually associated with it. (You should see the list of people who claim to have been integral to the making of *The Office*, versus the list of people who laid claim to it when it was first broadcast.)

'How has the show been for you?' asked the man, who looked and smelled like someone in a fragrance advert. I knew what he expected me to say – what the Mark Watson of most of this book would have said. 'Oh, not bad, a bit hairy when I nearly slammed us into another car, a little bit stressful when I kept having panic attacks at the wheel and your man responded by getting me to drive faster and faster – but thanks for having me on the show!'

'I've been treated like absolute shit,' I heard myself say. 'This is the worst I can remember being treated on a TV show, actually, and that really is saying something.'

The exec blinked repeatedly, as if something was in his eye. Nobody had ever been rude to him before. Why would they? They all wanted to work in television.

'Right,' he said, 'I'm sorry to hear that feedback.' The word 'feedback' is a drug to people in his industry; if they can use it ten times in a day they go home happy. 'Can I ask what that feedback is based on?'

It felt disingenuous, at best. He'd been told I was such a wreck at the steering wheel that I had almost crashed; if he'd had to guess which part of my experience was unsatisfactory, that would have been a good place to start. I reined in my temptation to be sarcastic or swear at him again. I didn't think it was very realistic for me to pass a driving test in these circumstances – not in a week, very possibly not in a year. And that I thought it was irresponsible to the general public to have a show premised on the idea of nervous people shuttling up and down motorways as if they were dodgems. And that, on the whole, I thought it would be a good idea if they let me leave the series.

The exec – understandably – started to mutter about the contract and the difficulty of paying me in full. I began using phrases like 'in good faith' and 'I think you could do without the bad publicity', the sort of things someone with more self-possession and a network of lawyers might say.

I called my agent. I shouldn't feel as vulnerable at work – physically – as I did here, and I shouldn't feel as useless at the job, either. Of course, I *was* useless given the set-up they had in place, but that merely reflected the fact that

– to quote the refrain from earlier – I shouldn't have been there. And this time, I was brave enough to recognise that and to vocalise it. A brief conversation later, I was *not* there anymore. I had left a TV show midway through – not for health reasons as on *Celebrity Island*, but purely as a point of principle, for the first time in my career. A few years before, this would have felt like anything but progress. And yet it was. It really was.

'You're useless, mate.'

And so here we were again.

This wasn't quite the same situation as the driving show. Here, I *was* in my rightful environment. The issue was definitely with him, not me. But it boiled down to the same thing: I was being made to feel inadequate because of the unreasonable things that someone else wanted from the occasion. The driving-show people had wanted drama, mishaps – fodder for their 10pm time slot. This guy wanted whatever it is that people want when they make a spectacle of themselves during a public event. The feeling of being top dog; a moment in the spotlight. Whatever it was, I would probably have let him have it, at my own expense, at most points over the past decade and a half.

'You're useless, mate.' Imagine being told in public that you have no purpose – that you might as well not be there – by a man who works in an office with whiteboard graphs of coffee bean sales, who owns a T-shirt that reads 'ONE TEQUILA, TWO TEQUILA, THREE TEQUILA,

FLOOR', who hasn't bought a new album since the Dido one with 'Thank You' on it but has a Spotify account so he can listen to playlists when he's bench-pressing. Of course, none of these make *him* useless, either. Nobody is 'useless'. It's a disgusting thing to say and my disgust made me reach for some colourful language.

'You're being a bit of a count, mate,' I said – or very nearly that, give or take a vowel. That word, again; just like in Kent, all those years ago. But that had been a comedy club, this was a gathering of business people. A sort of gasp-giggle went through the second-rate hotel ballroom, a place that had not seen language like this since – well, probably the previous night when the waiting staff discussed the delegates at the last dinner like this. The guy asked me to repeat myself. I was now, truth be told, somewhat in two minds about whether it had been quite the right choice of words, but it isn't the sort of thing you can easily take back. Nor did I feel that I should have to, of course. Not this version of me. Not anymore.

I repeated my insult of choice, and elaborated. 'I don't think you're behaving much like a professional – in front of all your colleagues, and everything. I mean, other people seem to be enjoying it. It might not be for you, which is fair enough, but just show some basic courtesy. Turning your back like that and insulting me, at a fancy dinner where all you've got to do is listen for a bit . . . yeah, I think these are the actions of a prick.' I downgraded the insult for this third airing, but it was fair to say the horse had bolted, galloped around the field and was now taking a long piss all over the man's table.

The atmosphere in the room – reasonably flat and benign before – was suddenly febrile. People were laughing, clapping, whistling. The villain – or victim's – wife got up from her table and left. The man stayed where he was and I went on with my comedy routine to an enhanced, but nervy, reception. At the end, the applause was a bit livelier than usual for a corporate setting; several people came up and expressed their support. There were selfies. I felt like a minor celebrity, someone who'd been caught up in a scandal and come out the other side. I wouldn't have been amazed to come into the hotel lobby – which I entered fairly briskly, thinking there was no pressing need to hang around – and find representatives of the *Daily Mirror* offering to serialise my life story (this did not transpire, incidentally; for the avoidance of doubt, that's not how this book came about).

My welcoming committee in the foyer was a little less welcoming. The man's wife was there. She pointed dramatically at me, as if I were the aggressor. 'How dare you!' she shouted. I couldn't remember the last time anyone had said, 'How dare you?' and not to me; it was the sort of thing teachers used to shout at the braver, naughtier kids at school, the ones who went into chemistry lessons with an active agenda of blowing things up, rather than just half an eye on that as a side benefit. She went on, 'How dare you humiliate my husband like that?'

I explained that I didn't really see it as having 'humili-ated' anyone. He had, if anything, been trying to do that to *me* and I'd defended myself. A comedian will always defend himself in that situation, I pointed out, and besides I hadn't said anything specific about him; I'd just called him a name.

'He's a good man,' said his wife, furious, 'he's a good man.'

I certainly should have walked away at this point. But my blood was well and truly up by now; I was surfing the wave of my bold response, of the way I'd looked after myself and, like a real surfer, I became filled with hubris and launched myself at a bigger wave while wear-ing indefensible clothes. 'I don't think he *is* a good man,' I said.

'How *dare* you?' she said, again, the 'dare' this time reaching the volume level hit by my old English teacher Mr Halls when a boy named Paul threw an apple out of a window. 'I have been married to him for twenty-five years.'

'Well, I don't think it was a good choice,' I said, saun-tering off to the lift and back to the hotel room I'd been given until midnight – corporate-booked comedians tend to resemble Cinderella in this regard, ceasing to exist after their performance. There, I looked out over the jumbled skyline, the London rooftops in the dark, thought about the very different landscape of the island, a nice, safe five thousand miles away, and congratulated myself, not just on a job well done, but a life, a personality, that had been completely turned around.

Was it a job well done, though? Am I really going to leave this penultimate chapter by saying that if you manage to gather enough self-regard, one day you too can be rude to a middle manager and his wife in a past-its-best London hotel? Or that, if you are pushed hard enough, you will eventually find the courage to say, 'I don't want to drive a car at a speed that is too dangerous for my ability anymore'? No. I'd be disappointed, after all this, if you thought those were my points. Even though both of these stories end relatively well for me, we learn as much from what I did wrong as from what I did right.

It wasn't that I got into any trouble. The coffee client was very supportive, in fact. They not only sent their apologies for the conduct of the executive, but enough free coffee to make me want to leap into the English Channel and try to swim across. There were no professional repercussions and I never heard from the man or his irate wife. I also didn't suffer any long-term damage as a result of withdrawing from the driving show, because not many people watched it and it was not recommissioned after the second season – not, as one might hope, because everyone concerned went to prison, but simply because of the changing fashions of TV. No, the trouble I had to face was all in my head.

Really, did I have to be so confrontational that both the coffee man and his wife would look back on the evening with regret? Did I have to make a woman I didn't know accountable for the behaviour of her husband? Did I even have to make such a fuss of it that, in my increasingly regretful memory, it virtually added up to bullying the guy in front of his workmates? It was right to stand my ground, but it wasn't right to trample over someone else's. I'd gone from one extreme to another.

And even with the driving show, should I have disrupted someone else's project like that, when I knew all along, deep down, that I wasn't a remotely suitable person for it? Wouldn't it have been better to show backbone earlier and turn down the invitation altogether? Alternatively, wouldn't it have been professional to plough on, improve, confront my fears, and – in the series finale – dramatically pass the driving test by getting a body double to do it for me, rather than flouncing off in a way that probably caused stress and trouble for a number of others? In short, was there not a way I could have achieved these apparent personal breakthroughs without ruining somebody else's day?

You can see the point: the more I ran these supposed victories through the courtroom of my mind, the more they began to feel like provisional victories at best; victories that were bound up with the need to defeat someone else, that relied on a kind of behaviour that I didn't particularly want to be associated with. Does this mean I was wrong to see them as steps forward or to see myself as having progressed? No. It's just that we need to come back to our friend from a long time ago, The Fallacy of Victories and

Defeats as a Way of Looking at Life. He's got a convoluted name, our old friend. But he's got a point, all the same.

A lot has changed for me, both internally and in professional terms, since my hurried escape from Maidstone. (Even Maidstone itself has changed, you'll be gratified to hear: I went there on my tour in spring 2022 and found the audience delightful. It wasn't the original venue, of course; I heard that burned down.) The business, however, remains as capricious and punishing as it always was, and it would be dishonest to claim that I always deal better with those punishments than I used to in the early days.

When I began writing this book a couple of years ago, I was chest-deep in one of the most demanding and exciting projects of my entire career. I'd been approached to write the script for a film adaptation of a novel. It would star, and be directed by, one of my favourite actors – a major Hollywood name, by any measure. It was the sort of opportunity I had dreamed about for a long time, and it came about because the novel (a sort of middle-aged romcom about lost and found love) contained similar themes to a radio play I'd written. I was summoned to pitch to the famous star and her producer. Because the level of her fame was too great to meet in a public bar, I was texted the number of her hotel room and asked to delete the text afterwards. I arrived approximately an hour early and paced around the foyer, presumably looking like exactly the sort of stalker these precautions were designed to weed out. At the right time I knocked on the door; the producer opened it; there, implausibly, sat the woman I had been admiring on screen since 1995.

Over the next hour, things went better than I could even have daydreamed. The celebrity and her right-hand man talked enthusiastically about the sample pages I had sent; they asked all about my career, though we didn't get on to the bit where I crashed a motorbike into a wall. At a certain point, the A-lister opened the minibar, and finding it empty she called down for champagne. She opened the champagne, poured everyone a glass and said: 'I'll put my cards on the table: I would love you to be my writer.' None of this was done in an apparent attempt to dazzle me or show off. Actually, one of the things I'd always loved about this film star was that she'd always seemed so measured and unpretentious. To have my admiration vindicated, to find her exactly as I hoped she would be, was a joyous experience. To have her call herself a 'fan' and to invite me formally into a potentially life-changing collaboration: you can imagine I felt even less internal composure than I am noted for. I walked away from the Soho hotel in a happy daze (not alcohol-induced; I'd barely dared to drink a mouthful in case I ruined the moment somehow). Was this too good to be true?

Well, no. An official contract arrived and was signed. I threw myself into the work, producing a full draft within three months as directed. I was given notes, wrote another version, attended a lunch with the famous actor and various other members of her team to discuss the next steps: this took place in an establishment so fancy that when the maître d' offered to take my coat, I declined, feeling it was some sort of income assessment I was likely to fail. I wrote a third version of the script, confident that the notes were sparking improvements each time. I was new to this discipline, after all; I deferred gladly to people with more experience. What I felt I could contribute was comic writing and character insight; half my life had been spent honing those skills. Despite the many lessons about the fallacies of 'getting what you deserve in the end' and 'everything leading up to this' which I might have absorbed by everything else you've heard about in this book, I allowed myself to inhabit a mental universe where the film came to be a reality; where, maybe, I was invited to work on other things with this screen star and her associates, and – here, in the second half of my life – began to make the impact on the world I'd so often told myself was beyond me.

The global invasion of Covid-19 naturally derailed the film project, as it did almost everything, but I was led to understand it wouldn't be a permanent derailment. Actually, when I spoke to the producer in the lockdown, he was upbeat about the progress he'd continued to make in leading the movie closer to production. There was now a studio involved, whose name you would recognise from that bit at the start of any film where a series of elaborate logos flash up and you keep thinking the actual story has started. The names of potential cast members kept being thrown into discussions, all of them among the most famous actors in the world. The names seemed fanciful, of course, but they were no more fanciful than the one I had already met, drunk champagne with and was now able to correspond with by email (a privilege, to be absolutely clear, I did not abuse, however keen I was to ask whether she was watching *Squid Game* or had joined in the Wordle craze). There was a little lull as pandemic restrictions softened, because my celebrity partner naturally had a backlog of filming to attend to, but by the summer of 2021 the project was back on.

There was now, in fact, a new urgency to proceedings. The studio was keen to shoot a year from then; budget had been allocated, a schedule was being drawn up. This meant that a new, supercharged, this-really-is-it version of the script needed to be written fast. To help me, the producers brought on board an experienced screenwriter from Australia, where some of the film was set. They couldn't pay me for all the rewrites from this point, because the rest of the money had to go to hiring this guy and the many other things you need to get a film on its feet. My literary agent was understandably displeased by this, but I persuaded them to let me continue. We'd come so far. I could already see a version of the future where – perhaps at a writers' workshop, or even on the sofa of a chat show – I described how, yes, I'd taken things on trust, because I believed so much in what we were doing.

We were given three weeks to draw up this unsurpassable version of the screenplay. They happened to be the main three weeks of the Edinburgh Fringe, the busiest time of my year – and all the more so in 2021 given that we had lost the festival altogether the previous August. This, and the fact my new co-writer and I were on opposite sides of the globe, made it a daunting challenge. But, after all, this was the final chapter. I delved deep into my reserves of energy. We held Zoom writing meetings at the crack of dawn or at midnight. The Australian writer, Steven – also working at odd hours of the day – can fairly be described as a storytelling wizard. He showed me how to dismantle a story whose flaws had become invisible to me through overfamiliarity, and in a series of marathon sessions we built it back up. With this and my performing routine, I was now working eighteen-hour days and felt slightly unwell by the middle of the month, but it was a small price to pay. Everything was aligning. We delivered the script on time.

There was now a pause of a couple of months – perhaps odd, given the emergency-setting we had been placed on, but by now I was used to the fits and starts of this process and accepted them as an inevitable component of a job I was still learning about day by day. Eventually a creative meeting was scheduled. The famous actor had read the script and was delighted with it; she just had a handful of minor notes. The head of the studio, whom I now met for the first time via video call, redoubled the praise, while throwing in some suggested amendments of his own. There was a general consensus that the remaining work was pretty minimal, that we were very nearly there; but these tweaks did need to be made as fast as possible. Another reference was made to 'timelines'. Would it be possible to deliver one more version of the script by, say, this time next week? This was the week I was on holiday, staying with friends; the first holiday Coop and I had had since the pandemic began, and indeed one that had been deferred from July 2020. Nonetheless: of course. I set alarms and got up at 7am each day of the trip. I delivered the final, final script. I should say that I was not naive enough to think it would ever *quite* be final. We've all heard enough about movie production to know that tinkering continues, script changes keep being made, right up until the words are coming out of the actor's mouth (and, of course, even after shooting is done). But that was fine. I would rise to that, too. I was, in fact, psyched up by the idea. None of the broken projects of my past, none of the disappointments, would matter now. I'd made a breakthrough. It had taken me until the age of forty-two, but here we were.

It was now nearly Christmas. Having asked for this lightning rewrite, the studio head apologised that he wouldn't be able to read it because he and his family were going surfing. Fair enough. In the new year, the star emailed; she, too, had been very busy with family matters, but was very much looking forward to the read. The area of my diary they'd instructed me to keep clear for filming remained clear. I waited.

As I write these words, it is almost Christmas once more: a whole year has passed. I never heard a word from any of the people involved in the film again. The four years of development, the promises, vanished into silence. I asked a couple of times what was happening, to no response. The famous actor, of course, kept appearing in things; I have to see her face about once a month. The producer is still out there. The studio remains buoyant. Steven the screenplay guru will be working on a dozen other things. For me, it was as if none of it had ever happened. There was, and it looks increasingly certain there will be, no explanation. Either I was the victim of a (stupendously well done, and surely expensive) prank, or not one of the individuals with whom I collaborated from 2017 to 2021 considered me worth giving enough of a shit about that they would send even a text to let me know what happened, or just say thank you for trying.

I think about it every day, without wishing to, and I know that will continue for years. In the time I've been writing all this, among some real blessings and high points, life and work have delivered some of their usual round-houses to the soul – betrayal by a friend and colleague in whom I'd invested a huge amount of time and life; another three-year writing project snuffed out with barely more communication than I got from the film people; a series of snubs from former allies I asked to collaborate with me.

Each one of those blows has sent me back to thinking about the film, the happy ending that never was, and each time I hear that man's voice saying, again: 'You're useless, mate.'

But I'm not, not really. It's just that hovering above all the lessons I've tried to relearn by writing this book, there is a sort of uber-lesson: no matter how enlightened you become about the inevitability of mortification and disappointment, you'll continue to fail, to be disappointed *by* your failure, to put that wisdom into action. For all the things I've learned during my life's misadventures, I wouldn't say I have become a different, better, person. I've brushed up against truths, made temporary advances, relapsed again, got back up again. This might sound a discouraging note to strike, but I've come to think it's just what life is meant to be. Perfection is a cold, not very human notion – most of us agree on that. But we keep pursuing an endpoint, all the same, driving towards the moment where we can say, 'I got there; I've worked myself out.' The grand unveiling. We'd be better off seeing the whole dance from cradle to grave as a work in progress.

Comedians like to use the title 'work in progress' to mean a show that isn't quite finished yet but which we nonetheless have the audacity to charge the general public to come and see, because of delusions of importance, greed, etc. Some particularly cautious acts, myself included, have been known to keep the 'work in progress' title in place even after months of development, in an attempt to manage expectations and take the pressure off. I was once asked by a slightly hostile journalist why, in the field of comedy, people thought it was appropriate to advertise shows for sale which – by definition – we were essentially admitting were not yet fully ready for consumption. Part sincerely, part playfully, I tried to make a case that *all* stand-up shows should be billed as 'in progress', because as a live performer you're always reworking, always finding new ways to do things. The work evolves, over the course of months performing it, in a way that a book cannot: unless I go into every bookshop and make alterations with a biro, which I think is going to be more trouble than it's worth to spice up a couple of disappointing adjectives.

Life is a similar story. There is no point at which you step back from yourself, as if from a painting, and say, 'That's done, I'll take three grand for that, please.' There are, instead, constant re-evaluations, stumbles that you have to get back up from. Even the softest and cosiest approaches to self-help tend to talk about getting up each morning and trying to do a little bit better than the day before. And sometimes life won't even allow you *that* measure of encouragement. Some days, you get up and within an hour it's quite clear you are going to end up a bit worse off than yesterday. Some days you know within ten minutes. There might be days when you *don't* get up at all, although don't mention that in front of people with children.

I said at the outset that I'm suspicious of people who present themselves as having left behind their foolish old ways and 'grown' as individuals to the point that they have something to teach the rest of humanity. 'Life's a journey, not a destination' is very high up on the list of aphorisms that make the flesh crawl, for the usual reasons: our over-exposure to it, its tendency to sound like it's meant to be printed on a mug you received in Secret Santa. Or the family holiday memories it conjures of your mum saying, 'Well, it's nice to see somewhere new, anyway, isn't it?' as your dad takes you up the same French country lane for the sixth time and you start to wonder whether you will ever, in fact, see a destination at all. But if you can find a palatable way of phrasing it for yourself, it is worth bearing in mind.

The various little deaths that occur day-to-day don't mean *you* are dead, even if parts of what you wanted or hoped for have to be left along the way, parted with painfully, as has been the case for me. There is only one form of 'death', in fact, that can't be recovered from; that is, as far as we know, irreversible. I don't like to think or talk about it, or acknowledge it at all. But it frames everything we do. It is, of course, death itself. Something that appears not to be there for long periods, but which is, all the same, always getting a bit bigger and closer, like the storm clouds moving in their menacing way towards the island.

The sky's going dark outside. It's time. Get ready.

EPILOGUE:

LET'S DO IT TOGETHER

It's my final day on earth; the hours are running out. An unexpectedly large number of people have showed up at my house to see me off. Friends and loved ones, as you might expect, but also quite a number of people who have played only peripheral roles in my life, and I in theirs – characters I am somewhat surprised to be saying a proper goodbye to, in such an intimate way.

Exactly how this goodbye is going to be conducted, and even why, isn't completely clear. I mean, I'm not obviously ill; I'm not in bed, or anything. Nor am I in any sort of imminent danger, that I can see. I'm only forty-three, and however poorly I might have looked after myself at times – well, forty-three is 'no age at all', as people say when somebody's time on the planet comes to a premature end.

I am bustling around my house exactly as I did at other parties I hosted during my decades of adult life: making sure my visitors have got drinks, are having a good time, are aware that I'm grateful they made an effort. So, yes, when pushed, I can't really tell you why this party has been thrown to declare the end of my life. But that *is* what's happening. Guests keep referring to it, some in quite emotional terms, as seems appropriate; others rather flippantly, with that 'we've all got to go *some*time' vibe that many people are surprisingly able to adopt. And the moment is getting closer: as with the chimes on New Year's Eve, there is a sense of a collective countdown. Within an hour, maybe less, I will have said 'farewell' forever; I will be dead.

And then, before it can actually happen, I wake up, clammy and tousled in the sheets, my heart racing, the familiar surroundings of the bedroom gradually taking over. I understand that this was all a dream, one that's been recurring for well over half my life. The first time it happened I was sixteen and the dream was so vivid and played out in such convincing detail that I was physically drained by the experience and walked around school all day with the memory of it in my bones, only half able to believe that I had escaped and I wasn't merely trudging around some afterlife – in which, oddly, I still had double physics first thing on a Friday morning.

As the years went by and the dream started to get occasional reboots, like a play being staged with different casts, I reached a point of familiarity with it. Even as it was happening I *half* knew I was participating in a dream; that I wasn't going to die at the end of this sequence. These days it's almost like a classic episode of something that always comes round at Christmas or on a bank holiday. I think, Ah, it's this one again. I am still tachycardic and breathless when I wake up; I still shudder with a full-body relief that I have escaped, all over again. But the dream has lost its power of shock, the sensational intensity it had when it was premiered.

Is that good news? Not really. It isn't that I have become less scared of the events taking place in the dream or what they mean; the inescapable truth they point to. It's just that I've learned more about what dreams are, what psychic work they do for the brain in what is meant to be its downtime. I know that I have a recurring dream about the end of my life because, in my waking hours, I can't cope with the idea of my own death. I can't confront it head-on.

Without wanting to sound morbid, the subject is slightly more pressing than when the dream first occurred. At sixteen, I was well within my rights to scream – silently – 'I'M TOO YOUNG TO DIE!' Over a quarter of a century later, I can still make a case for that, but it's less robust. Death does come to people in their forties – indeed, as we all know, to people significantly younger. Even if it's not for a long time, the day *will* come, as in the dream.

Very likely I will not be at a party, surrounded by well-wishers handpicked from different phases of my life. Some of the characters in the dream might well baulk at an invitation like that in reality, quite understandably if they haven't seen me since they were my dentist thirty years ago, or now live in New Zealand.

In all probability I will die either in a hospital bed or – marginally more fortunately – at home with a small number of people that I've undertaken life's journey with. I will close my eyes involuntarily for the final time and that will be that. 'Goodnight, Vienna,' as my dad sometimes says, for reasons I've never actually known, and which feel a bit strange to google now after all this time, and in the middle of this fairly demanding piece of writing.

'You won't know anything about it!' That's what people always say. They mean it to be comforting, but in fact it pours salt into the wound. Because they're right: I *won't* know anything about it and then I won't know anything beyond it, forever, for the entire expanse of time that lies ahead. I will be nothing. I will not exist in any sense beyond the symbolic and only then for a short while. The thought is enough to make me feel physically sick. It has taken me nearly an hour to write these words – not so much to compose them but to type them and look at them on the screen. I tend not to reply along those lines when I'm at someone's house for dinner. I just murmur, 'You're right, I guess,' and look around the table to see how easy it'll be to top up my glass.

This is all a bit of a downer, isn't it? Most of the book has been about – at least metaphorically – returning from the dead. Picking yourself up and returning to the battle.

Rehabilitating your ego, your self-esteem, from the many blows it must withstand over the course of a life, any life, even one less dependent on acclaim than a life spent in the spotlight. Understanding the damage you are capable of doing to your own body and brain and finding ways to be gentler to yourself. Occasionally, perhaps, even standing up to physical danger, real or perceived. How it is possible to get back on your feet after every one of these battles, and be better for it.

The fact remains, though, that the final card the world deals you is always the end of the game and the world always wins. Unless you have a belief system that incorporates a fairly literal afterlife or you place enormous faith in cryonic freezing (which, you may not be too surprised to hear, I have done a fair bit of research into), a day is coming when you will experience a death from which you cannot return. You can survive all the other types of death in this book, but you can't do anything about this one. How are we meant to bring things to a happy ending?

Reminders of this final fate are never far away. These days, I live near a beautiful old churchyard, a lot older and grander than the one belonging to my childhood church, whose occupants were once entertained every Sunday by my gravelly voiced mentor, Jon. During one of the lockdowns, I was leading my children across it and my son enquired, without warning, 'Do you think you'll be buried or incinerated, when your time comes?'

I answered in a good-natured way that I'd probably be cremated, because – among other things – the lavish stonemasonry and the sheer *space* demands of those ancient memorials are requirements we've moved on from to some degree. Not least because, I suppose, there are a hell of a lot more dead people than there used to be.

We looked together in silence at the little village of the deceased, the gigantic slabs of stone, covered in ivy, each one a stand-in for what used to be a living person. My boy remarked how strange it was to think that all of them had been there all the way through the Second World War and even the First World War, and some for most of the time Queen Victoria was around, and so on.

My daughter, who is quite a bit younger, asked whether dinosaurs would have seen the gravestones. I said I didn't think so. I looked at the two people I have helped to bring into the world, with almost all their lives still in front of them, and – at least in that moment – felt confident that they would have a better, less neurotic relationship with the idea of death than I have. My son has only in the past couple of years started to develop an interest in the hereafter; in one of our first weeks of home-schooling during the pandemic, he asked me whether astronauts, while floating around in space, were able to 'sneak into heaven'.

The fact is, most people never seem to experience the fear of the abyss the way I do. I know people who are more scared of breaking their leg than they are of dying. To be honest, I probably know people who are more scared of the meerkats on that price-comparison advert. 'You won't know anything about it,' they say. That, though, is what's truly alarming about the thought. Challenging as my dealings with my brain have often been, parting ways with it is – literally – unthinkable. I *want* to 'know about' it, about everything, even if knowledge is sometimes painful. I don't want the party to end.

I have touched frequently, in this book, on the many times my life has not felt like a paradise and on the handful when I could even have lost my grip on it altogether. There might well be more times like that ahead. But there will be huge rewards, too: times when the view of a new city knocks the breath out of me, when my children put their arms around me and the pent-up frustration of a whole day's parenting disappears like mist, when it's warm outside in the evening and I've got a restaurant table to sit at, a nice glass of wine. If I make it to one hundred it's conceivable my football team will get good at some point. I would rather cycle between happy and sad times forever than not have *any* times. The knowledge that I'm going to run out of time on this astonishing planet, run out of opportunities to do and see the things on offer to us, is agonising to think about. Being here with such a limited lifespan – and that's if you're lucky – feels like being taken to Disneyland as a child and then being told you've only got half an hour until it's time to head home again.

Still, I'm unlikely to get a reprieve. However many light-ning bolts I might dodge in my life, something is going to get me one day. Death is, when it comes down to it, as non-negotiable as council tax and, unlike council tax, you can't water it down by paying it in monthly instalments (well, unless you choose to regard every month of your life as being a sort of down payment on eventual death, but even I am not quite that gloomy). No amount of whining about the inevitable is going to make it disappear, not in the end. There can be no section of this chapter – unlike the others – in which I come out the other side of the ordeal, derive lessons and put those lessons into the beyond. There is no 'beyond'. I have to grasp around in the dark to find those lessons *before* the thing happens. The question, then, is what can I learn from the people I see every day *not* being debilitatingly afraid of death – the people, to borrow the famous observation by Jerry Seinfeld, who are more afraid of delivering a funeral speech than they are of being the subject of the funeral?

One thing calmer, better-adjusted people often say in times of crisis is, 'One day this won't matter anymore.' It's a well-known technique, when you're panicking, to make yourself consider: will this be as important in five minutes? And how about five days? And then, five years? In rare cases, the answer to all three questions is 'Yes'. If you've just sawn your leg off in a chainsaw accident, for example, it'll certainly be smarting in five minutes, and it is reasonable to assume that you'll still be dealing with the repercussions in five years.

But the bulk of our experiences are far less significant than they seem to be in the moment we first apprehend them. Almost no news is ever as good or bad as it first sounds in our ears. When I came back from the island, I waded through three weeks of emails I hadn't been able to open, many of them marked 'URGENT'. It was a real lesson in perspective to see how non-urgent all of them had become, less than a month after they'd been sent. Some related to matters which had been dealt with by other people while I was cowering in various ditches, it's true; but most were simply never as critical as their senders would have you believe.

If you're anything like me, you even have mental footage of times you were very upset or panic-stricken to the point of illness and yet now you cannot remember the cause of those emotions. Many troubles come and go in life and, on the whole, they leave much less of a trace than you would think from the way we respond to them.

So, 'one day this won't matter anymore' is a reasonably robust rule for hard times. And if we scale it up, maybe there's a message for people like me about the way to be sanguine when thinking about death. Death is the ultimate clean slate, after all. There is nothing you can mess up so badly that it will still be a problem for you the day after you die. A hundred years from now a completely new set of people, plus Bear Grylls, will be inhabiting this planet of ours. The idea that your deeds will be irrelevant to them, invisible to them, is certainly frightening to the ego, but it can also feel like freedom. Perhaps this sense of life as a plucky quest littered with setbacks and failures and embarrassments is what can prepare us for the ultimate setback.

Imagine you *do* get to the age of a hundred and you finally feel that you have nailed absolutely everything. Life is perfect; you have everything you could desire, and limitless potential to get even more. You have mastered life so completely that you only have to snap your fingers and you could get anything, go anywhere, *be* anyone. Imagine you've got all that and *then* it's taken away by death. The loss would be literally unbearable. You would be heartbroken to give up your place in the world. It would be impossible to make any sort of peace with it.

Life isn't meant to be perfect, and we aren't meant to do it perfectly, because it isn't ours forever: maybe that's a working theory that somebody like me can use to face the idea of the end. None of our victories are permanent, but nor are any of our failures, disappointments, mortifications. Just as the idea of life as a series of goals or targets is flawed and can hold us back, so is the overarching notion – the one we all carry in the backs of our minds – that, when it's all over, we'll be given some sort of score out of a hundred, some final report card.

Nothingness sounds a bleak proposition, but it's also the biggest get-out-of-jail card there is. What would you dare to do, if you didn't let yourself be put off by the fear of failure, judgement, ridicule? Well, fast-forward far enough and there won't be any of that. Nobody will be able to hear the piece of music that your life became. It was just for you.

As is pretty clear by now, I don't find it easy to look at things this way. I'm always going to put pressure on myself to 'win'; always going to be a harsh judge of where I end up in relation to that – often meaningless – aim. I'm going to repeat some of the mistakes I've described in these pages again and again. When my life approaches its final chapter, that chapter will very likely be as full of fears and frustrations as the final chapter of this book. But I'm hoping that if I commit these words to the record now, I'll have them to look back on. And maybe they will be useful to other people, too. For example, those two children who gazed at the gravestones with me that day during lockdown.

You two, you won't be kids forever, and – although I hope it's a long way off – the day will come when I'm only marked by one of those slabs of stone or maybe a plaque on a bench or, I don't know, whatever you decide (I'd rather not be scattered at sea, if that's OK; I feel like that way I'd be drifting even further away from you). When I'm not able to scoop you up into my arms anymore or play board games on long Saturday afternoons or be exasperated by the places you manage to leave your coats, all you'll have is a bunch of YouTube clips of varying quality, the memories

I've managed to leave you with – and whatever I was able to write down, including this.

If you've made your way all the way through it: firstly, well done; my generation used to complain that yours had no attention span. You'll have read how much of what I attempted didn't work out the way I imagined, but in a lot of cases that was OK. That my life was always a kind of work in progress, something I tried to put together as I was going along, rather than something I properly planned for (this won't come as a huge surprise if you think back to that time I took one of you to school without any shoes on because I'd left your only pair in Pizza Express). That I made some of it work, and some parts I just had to improvise. And, whatever people might tell you, that might be how you end up living *your* lives, too. That's fine, it's more than fine, and I'm proud of you, wherever I am.

But if you're reading this three months after it came out, secretly, at midnight: please for the love of God go to sleep, there's school tomorrow.

I've said all along that this isn't meant to be a handbook, a collection of wisdom, or any sort of guide to living, so much as an attempt to make sense of my experiences on planet Earth so far and draw some lessons from them. I won't try to sign off with a grand summary of what you are meant to have learned or a list of ten things to remember every day, like some writers do at this point. I'll just say that there have been small deaths of all sorts for me in this book and there are bound to be more ahead: more disappointments, upsets, losses. But I will still be alive. And while that remains the case, I will consider it a privilege to stumble on, trying to make out the music and move along to it, heading cheerfully towards the unknowable.

Whatever anyone might tell you, that's all they're really doing, too. It's all we've got. Let's do it together.